FRACTIONS WORKBOOK
Grade 3 Math Essentials

Children's Fraction Books

BABY PROFESSOR
EDUCATION KIDS

Speedy Publishing LLC
40 E. Main St. #1156
Newark, DE 19711
www.speedypublishing.com
Copyright 2016

Tell what fraction of
each shape is shaded.

Pie Shapes

Set 1

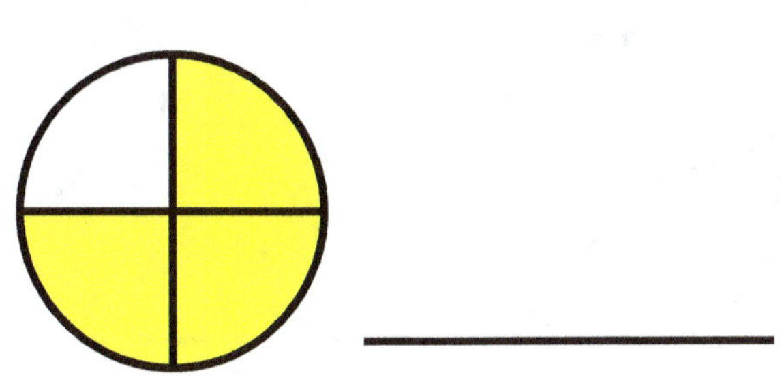 ________

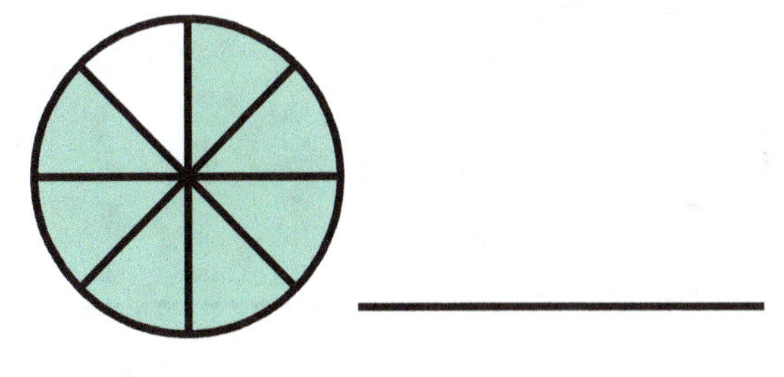 ________

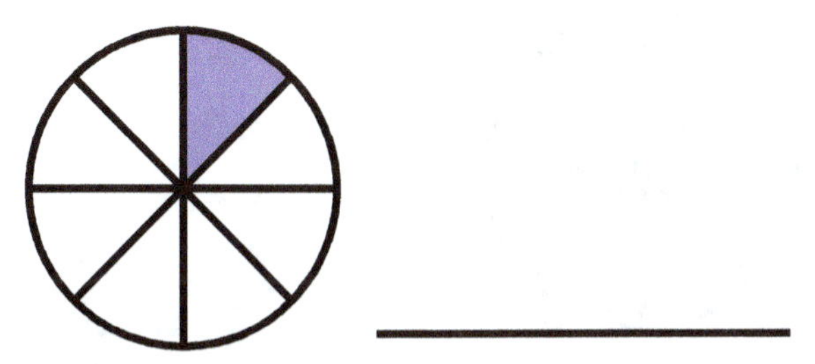 ________

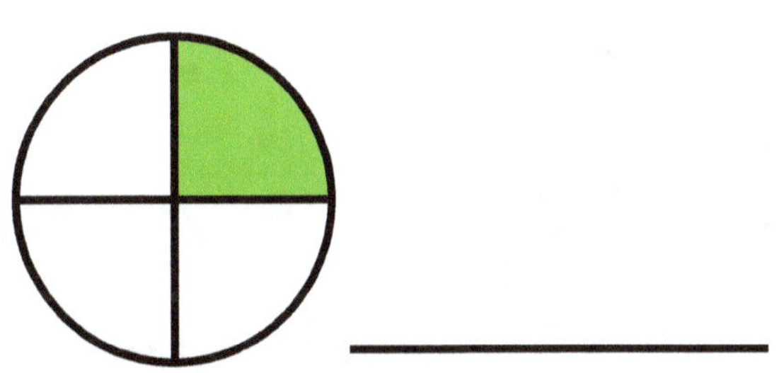 ________

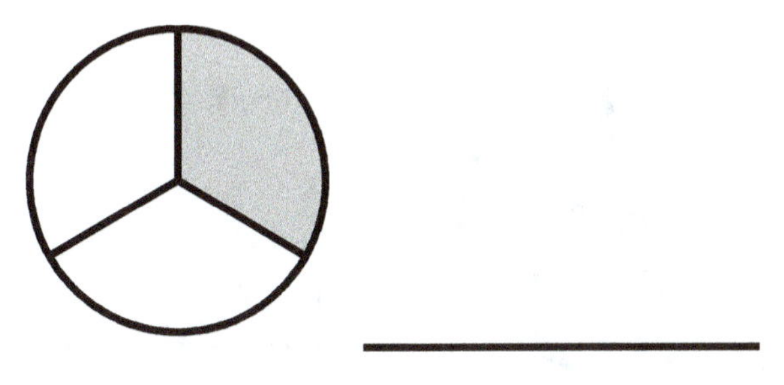 ________

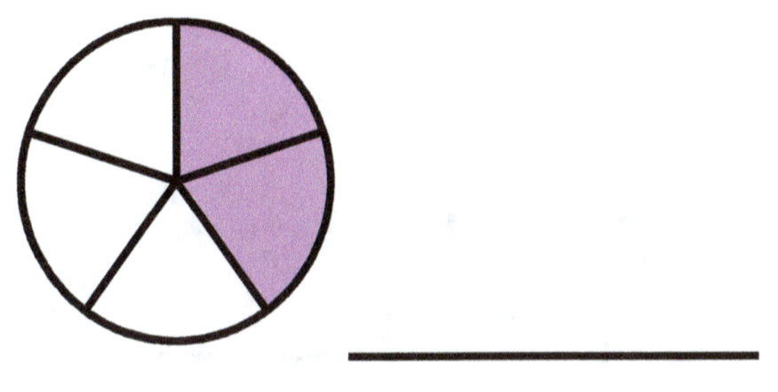 ________

Set 2

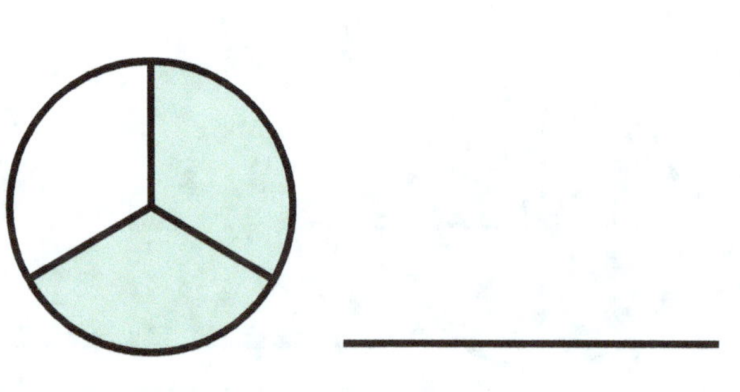 _______

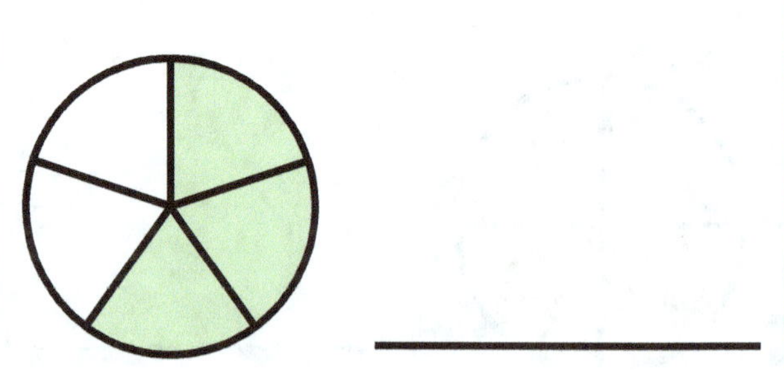 _______

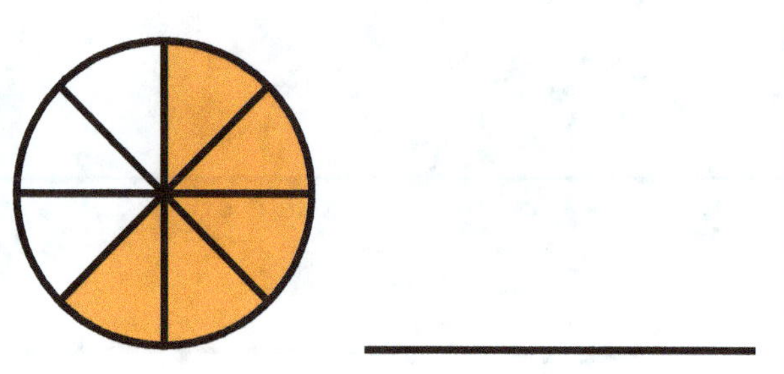 _______

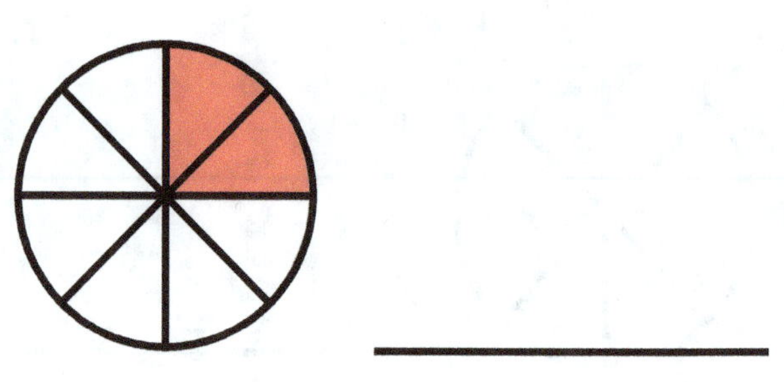 _______

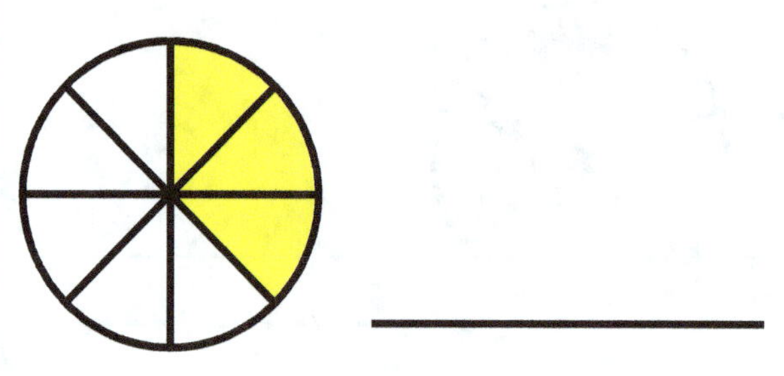 _______

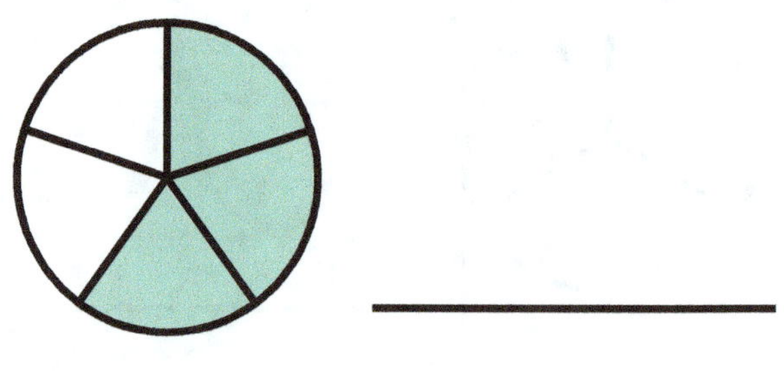 _______

Set 3

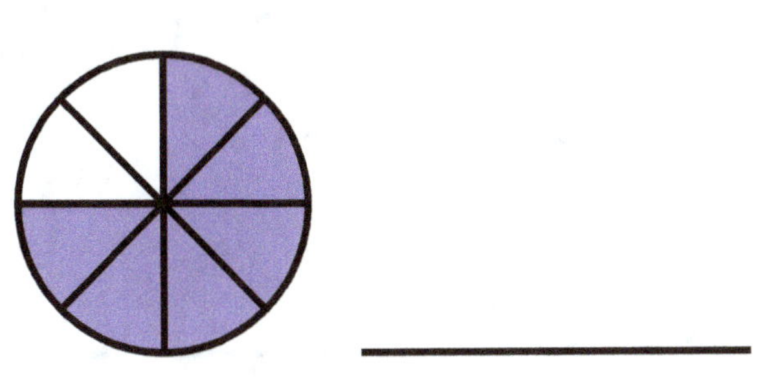 ________

 ________

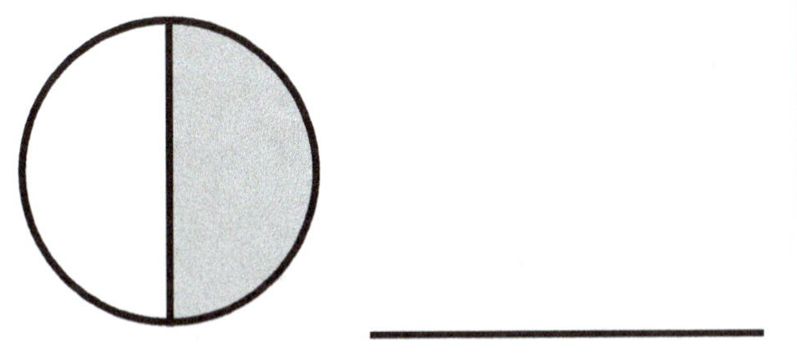 ________

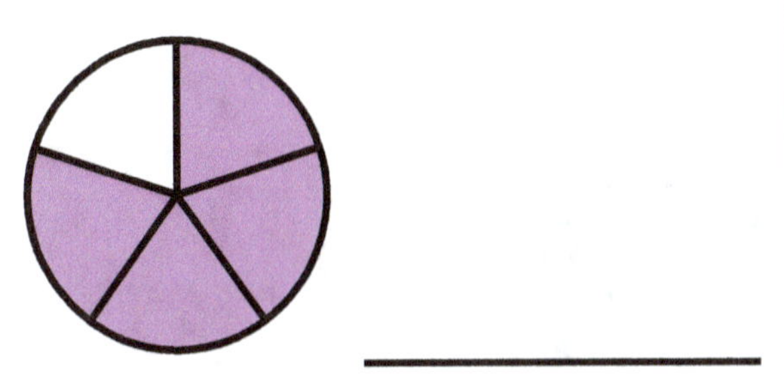 ________

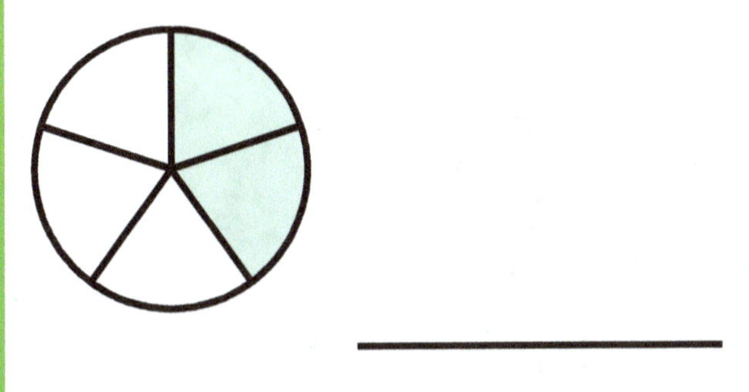 ________

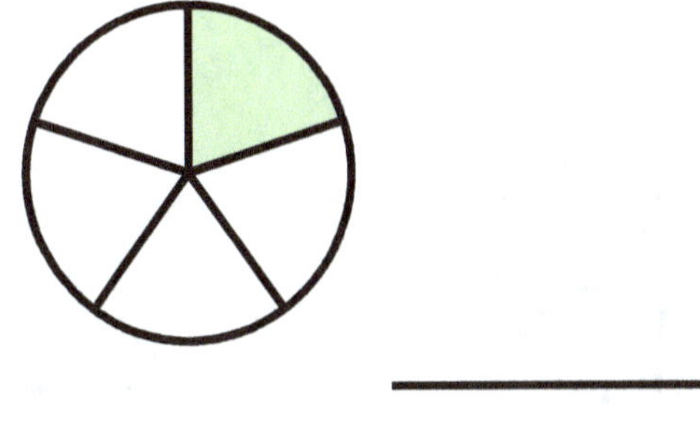 ________

Set 4

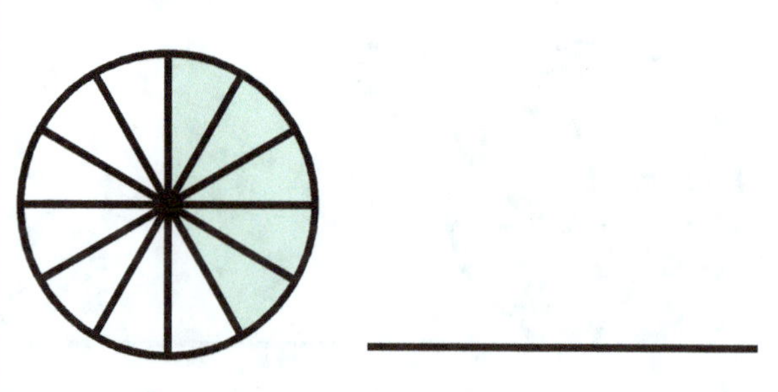 ____________

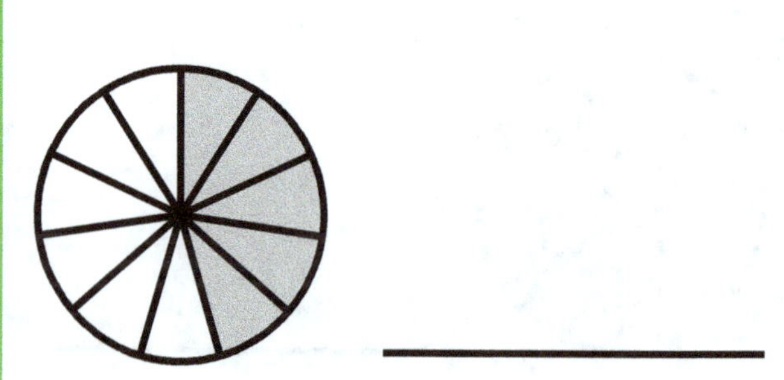 ____________

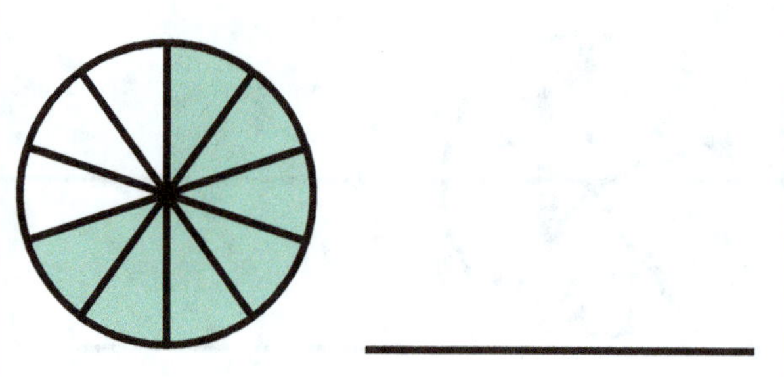 ____________

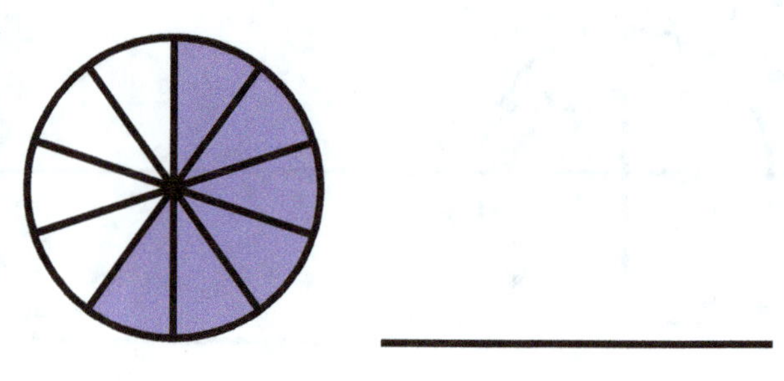 ____________

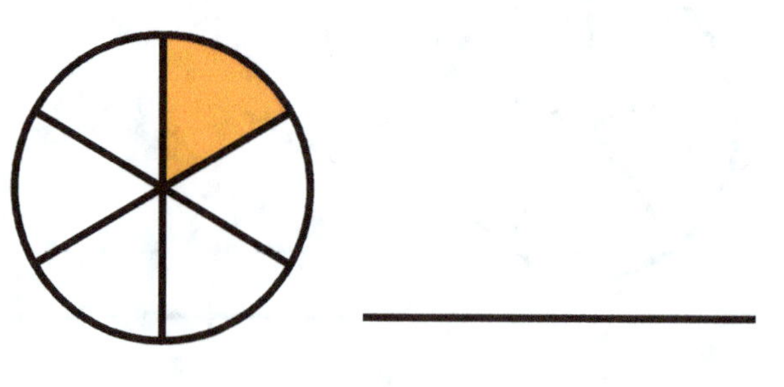 ____________

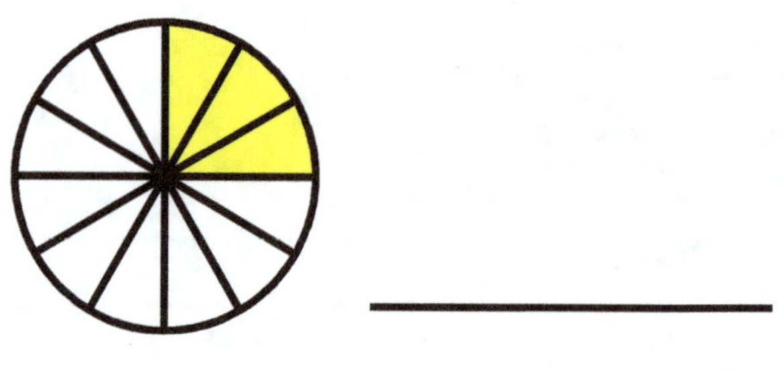 ____________

Set 5

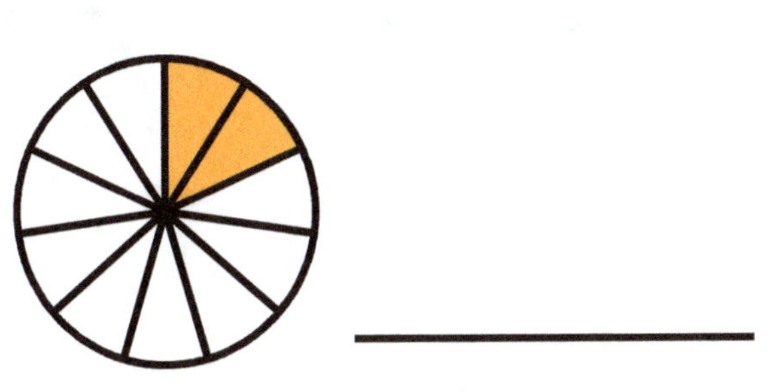 __________

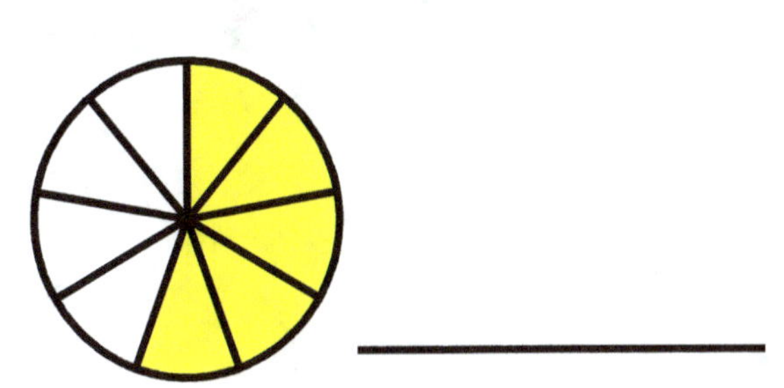 __________

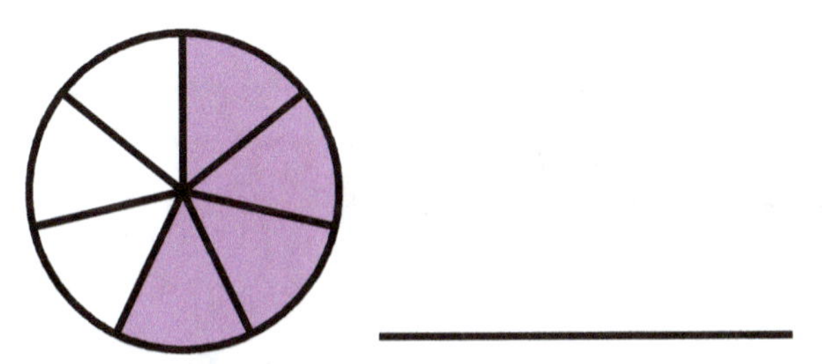 __________

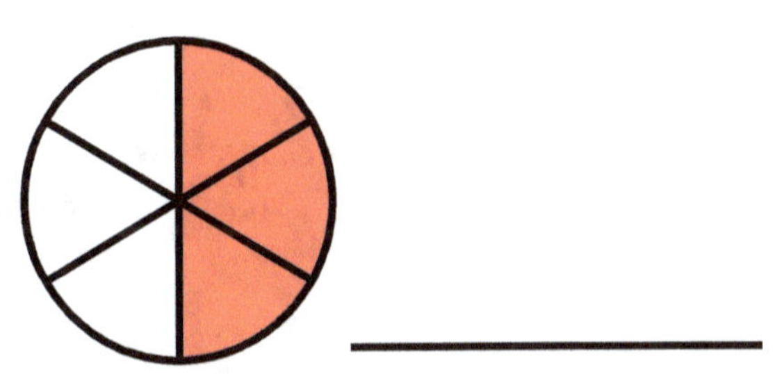 __________

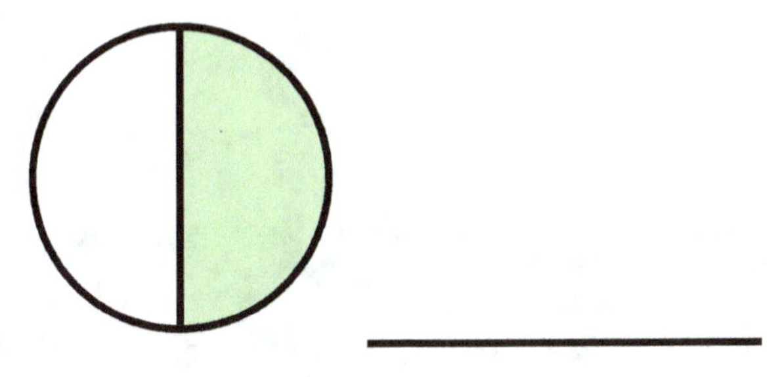 __________

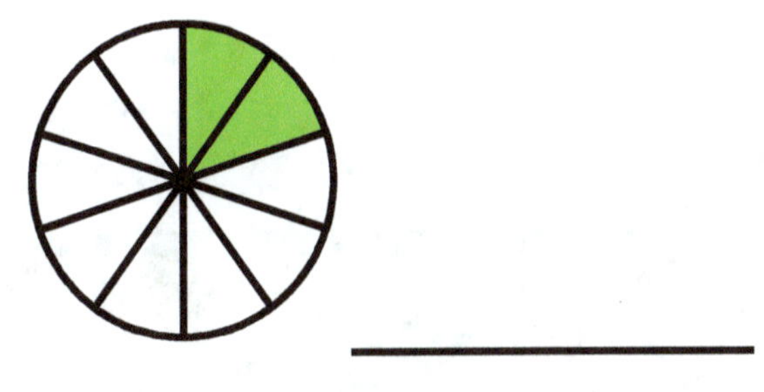 __________

Rectangular Shapes

Set 1

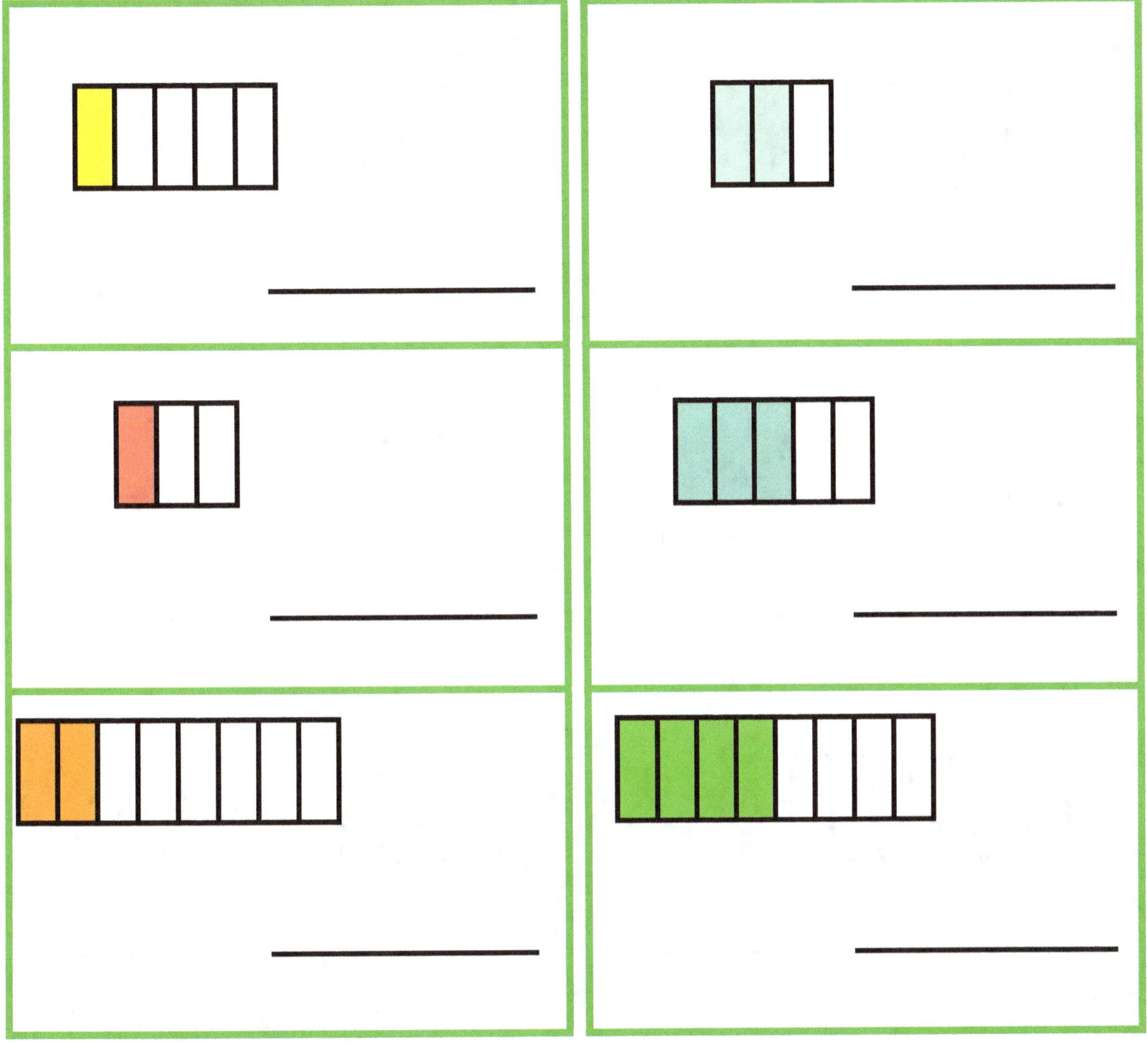

Set 2

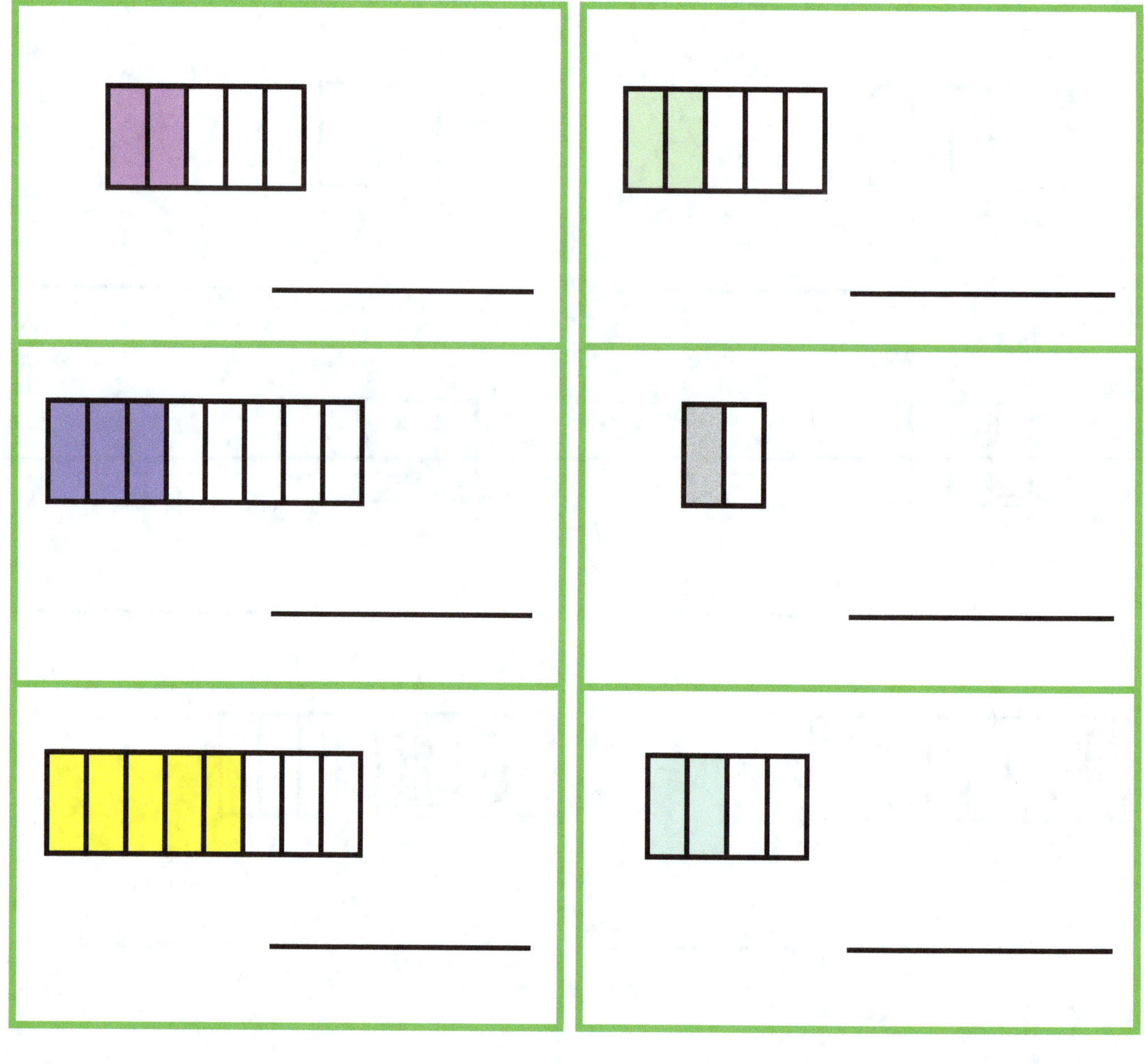

Set 3

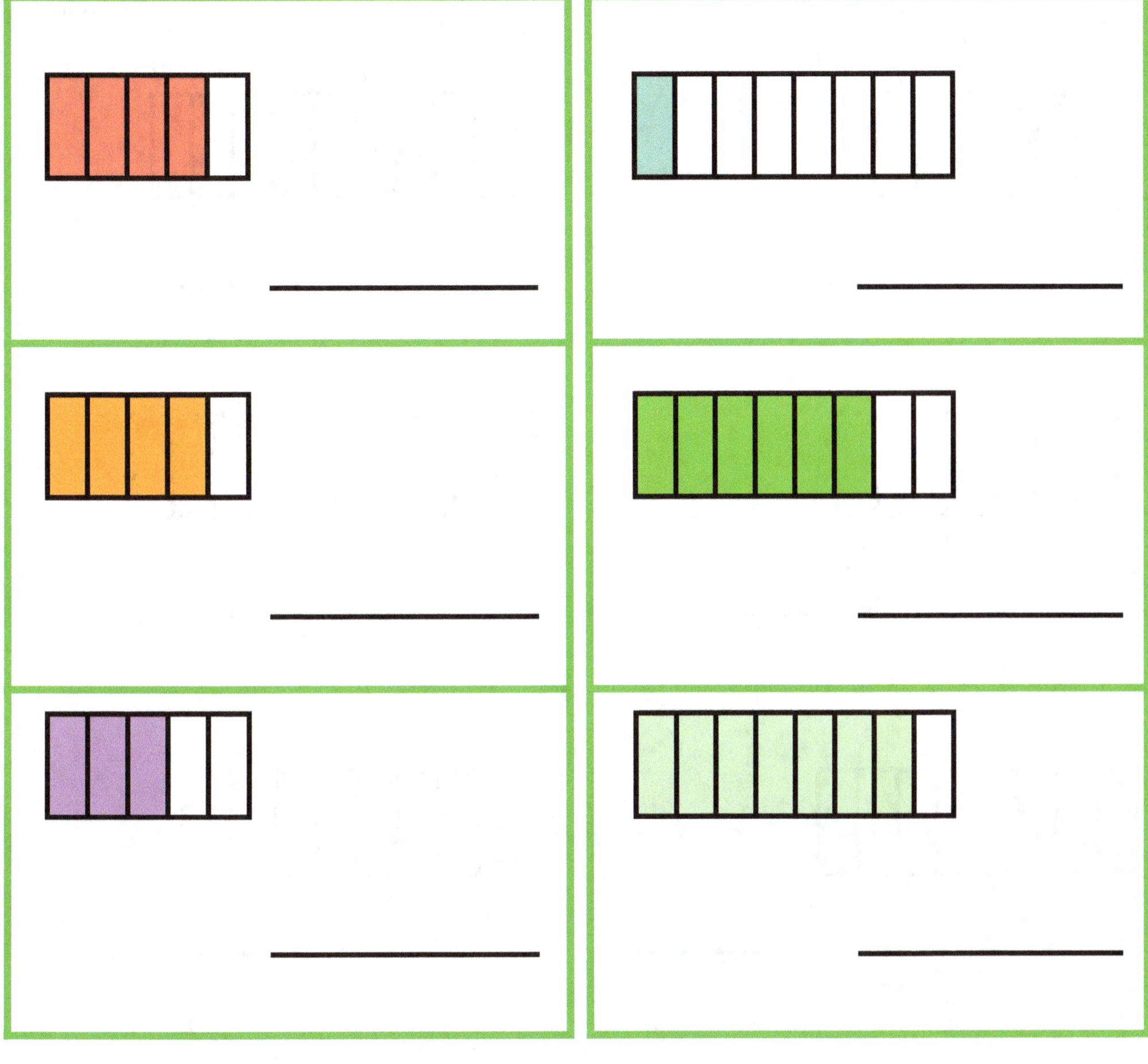

Set 4

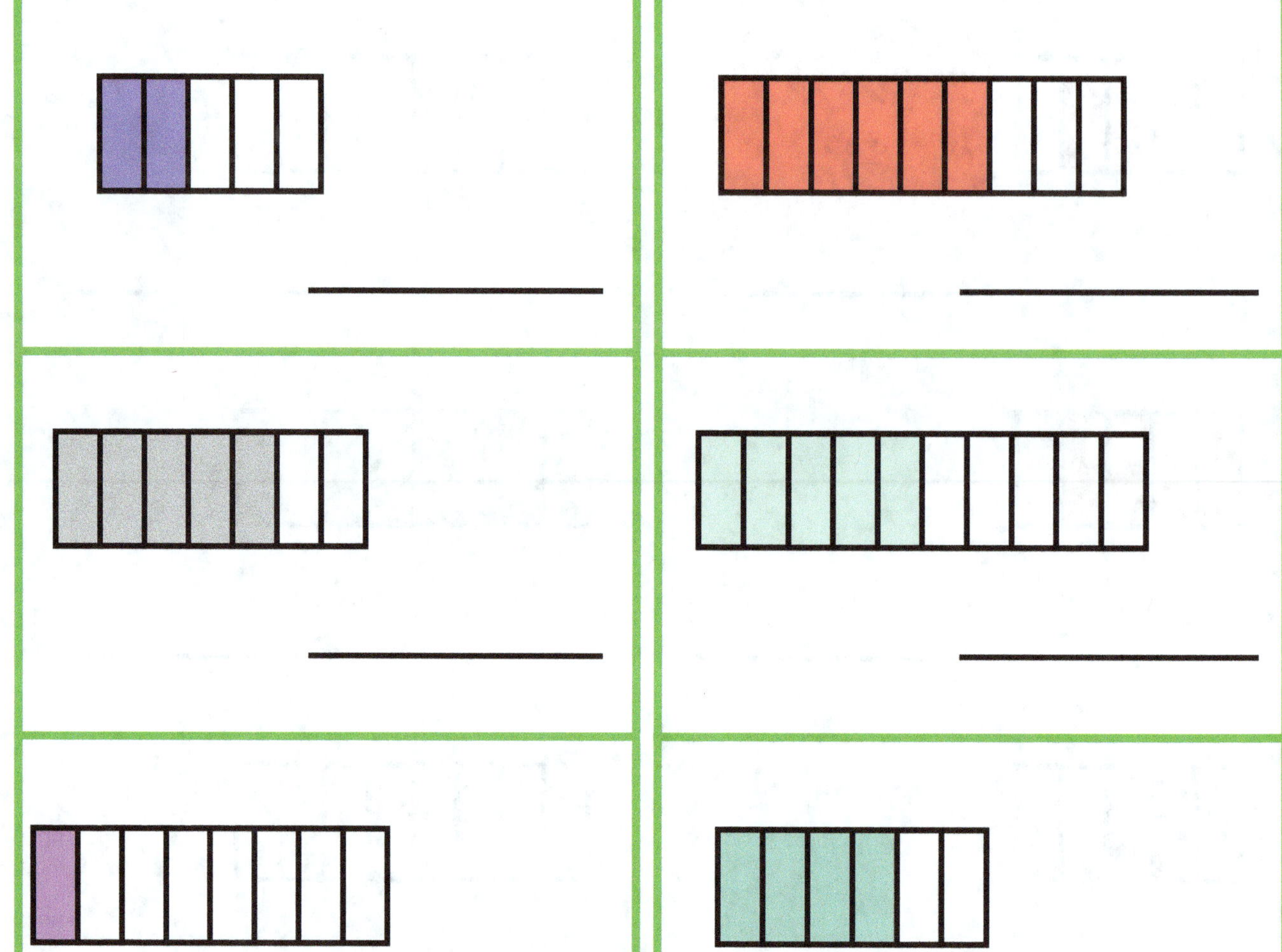

Set 5

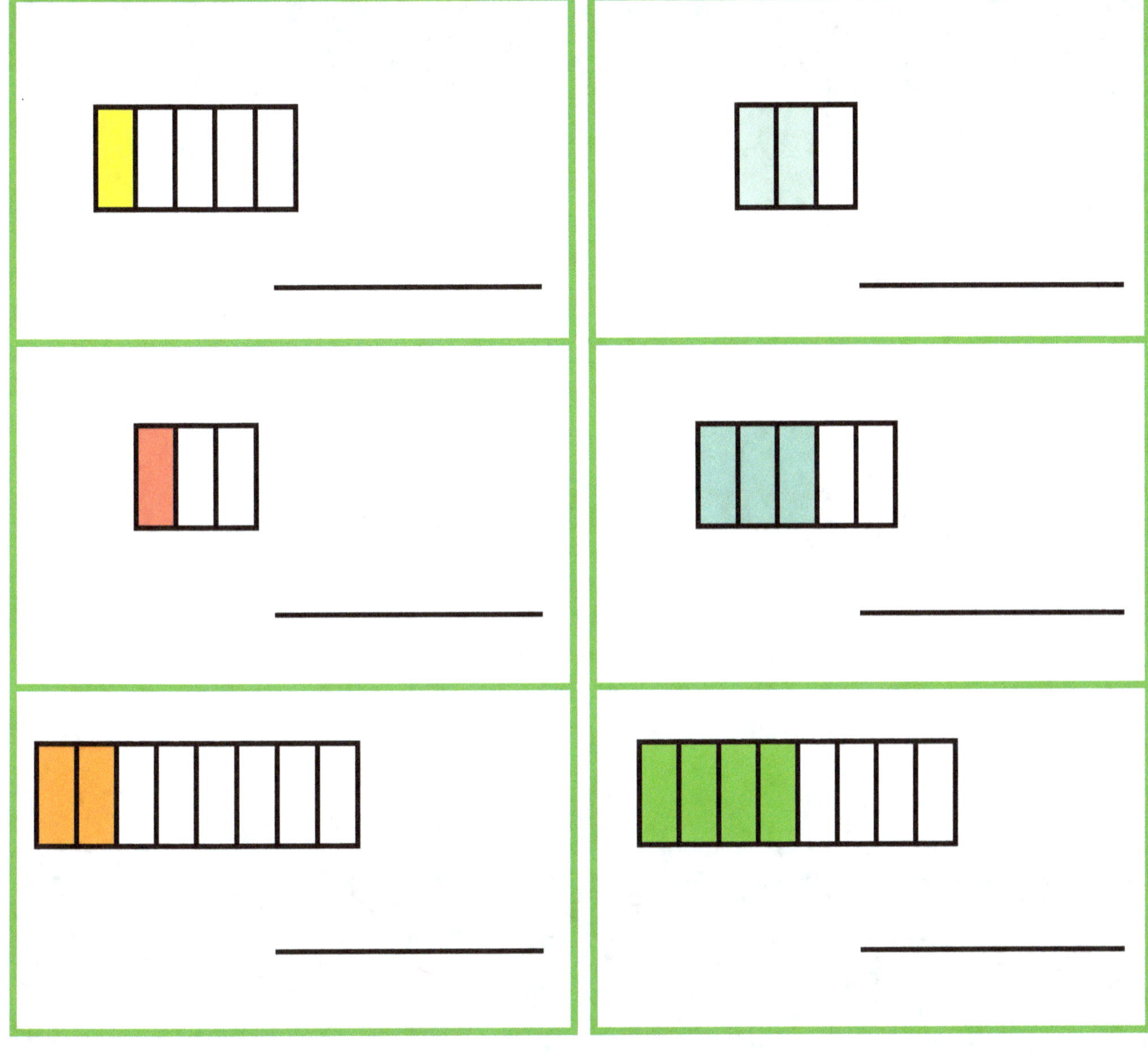

Polygonal Shapes

Set 1

 ___________

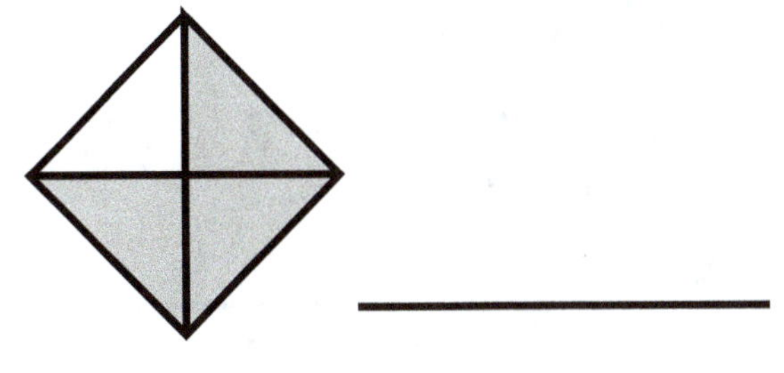 ___________

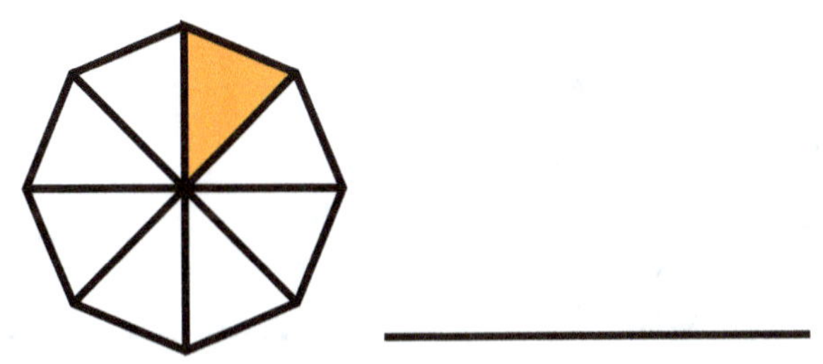 ___________

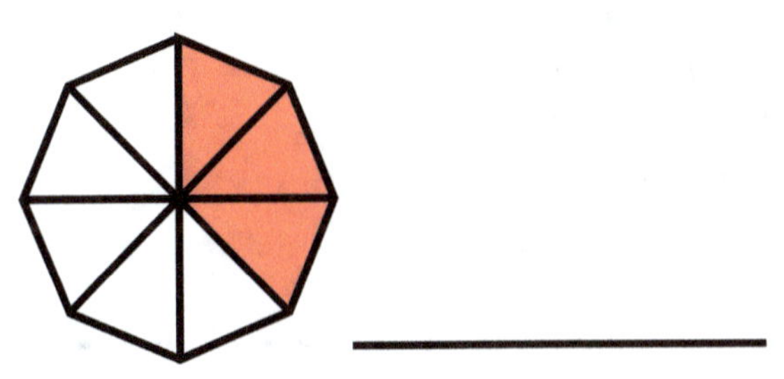 ___________

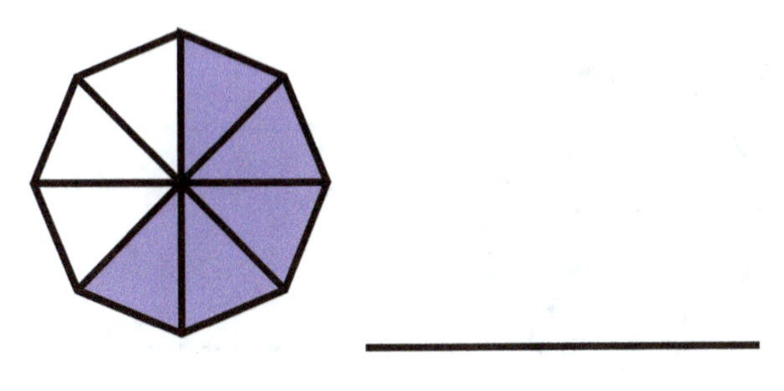 ___________

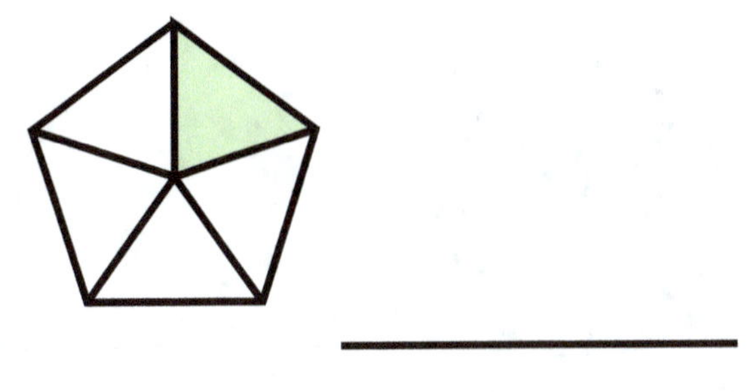 ___________

Set 2

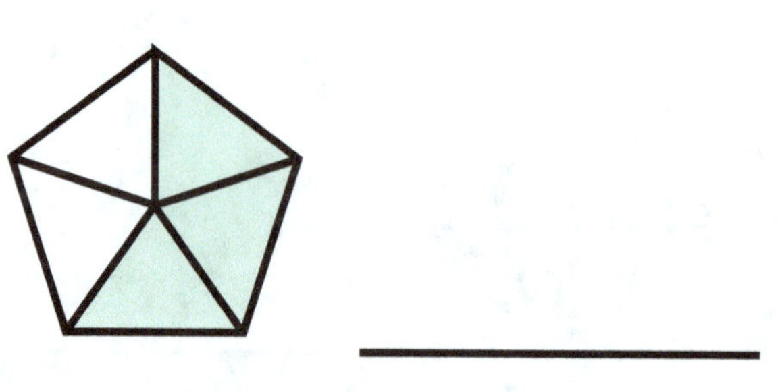 _______________

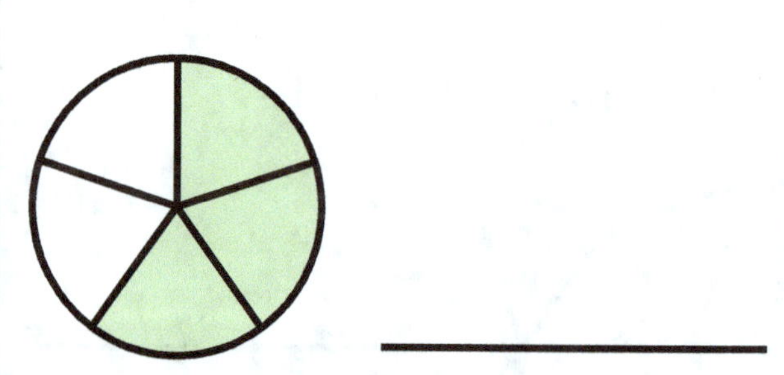 _______________

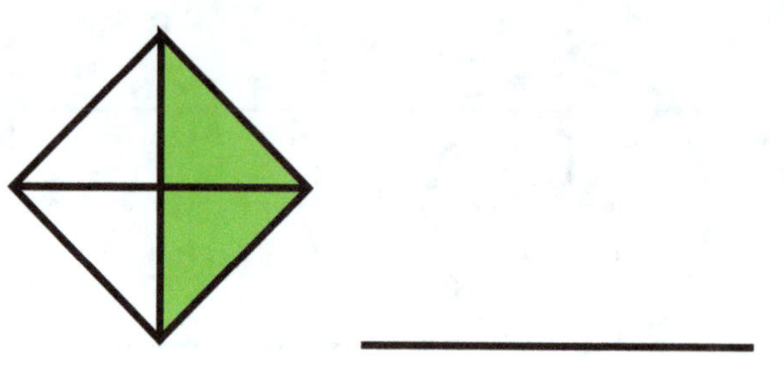 _______________

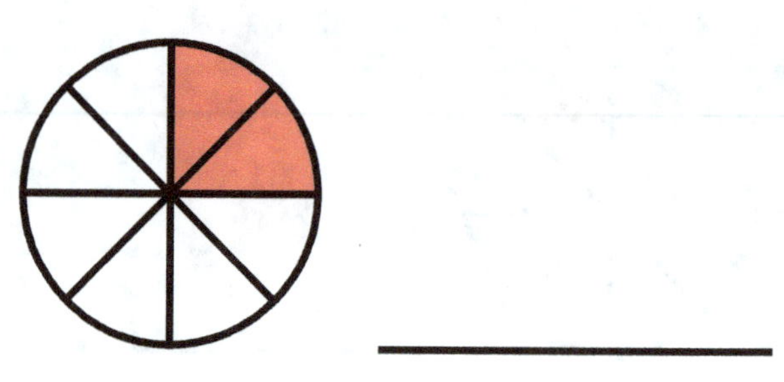 _______________

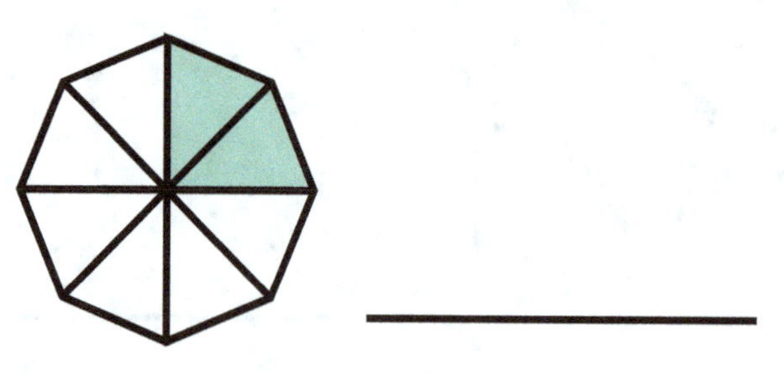 _______________

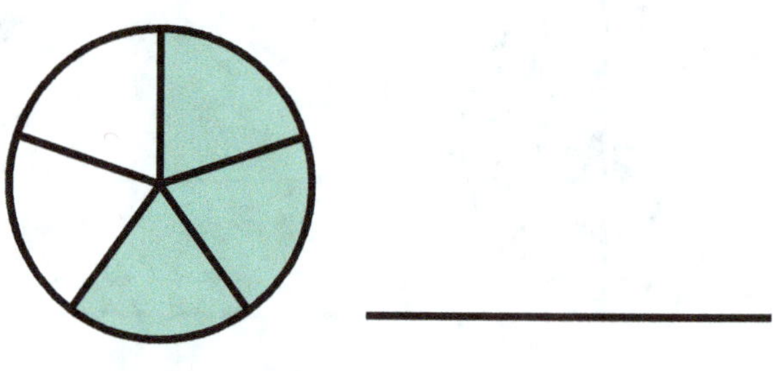 _______________

Set 3

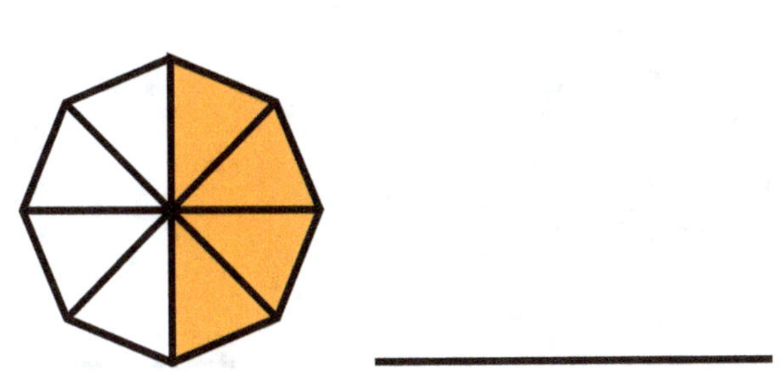 ________

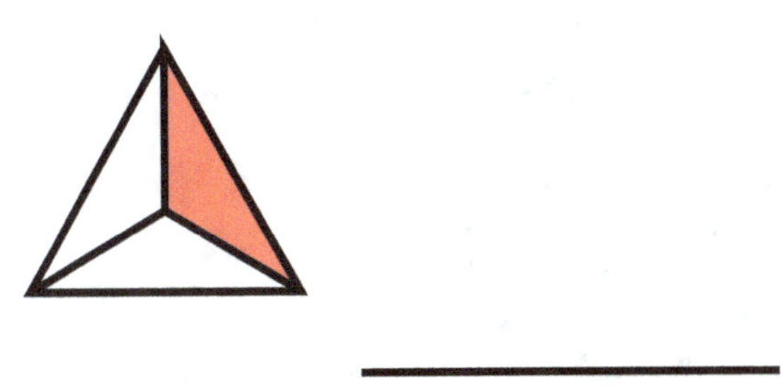 ________

 ________

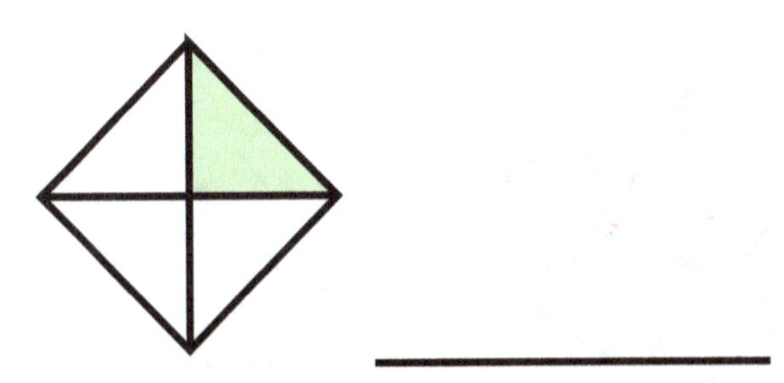 ________

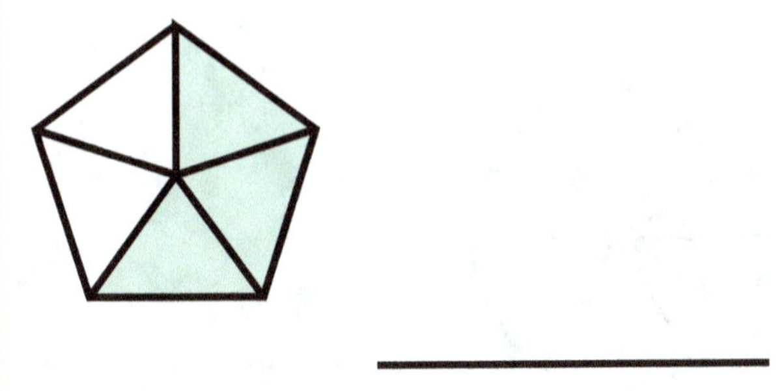 ________

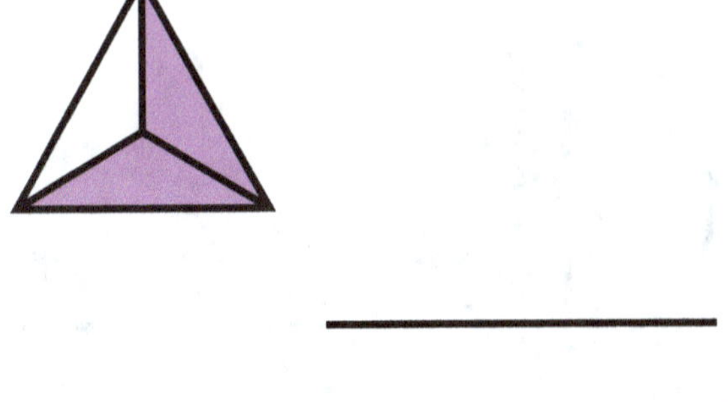 ________

Set 4

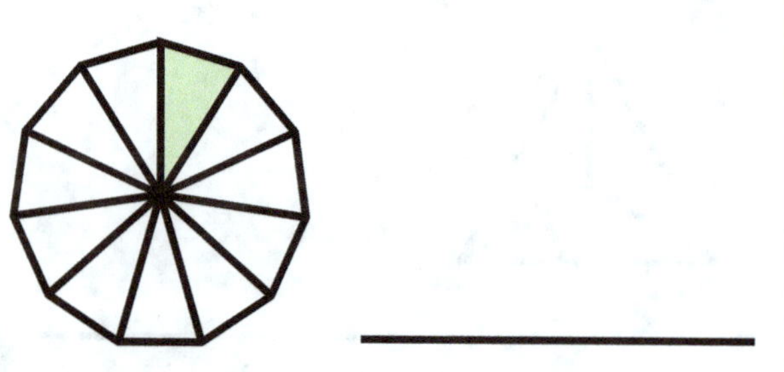
____

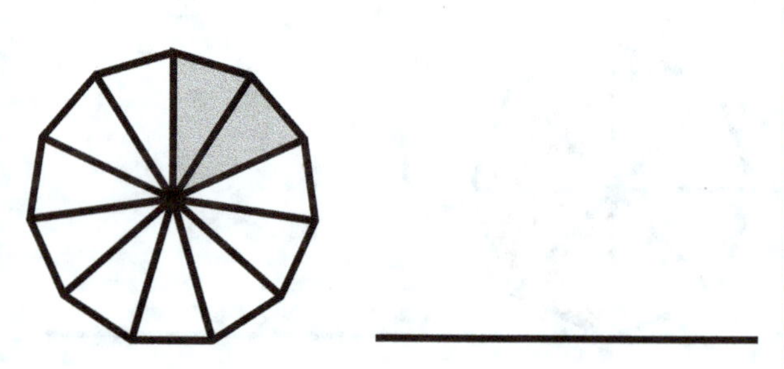
____

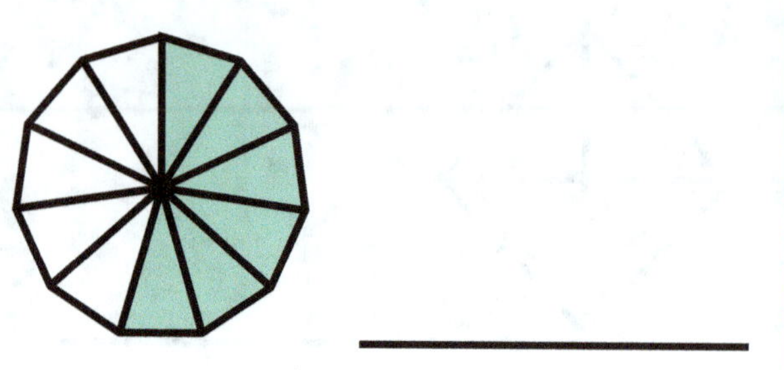
____

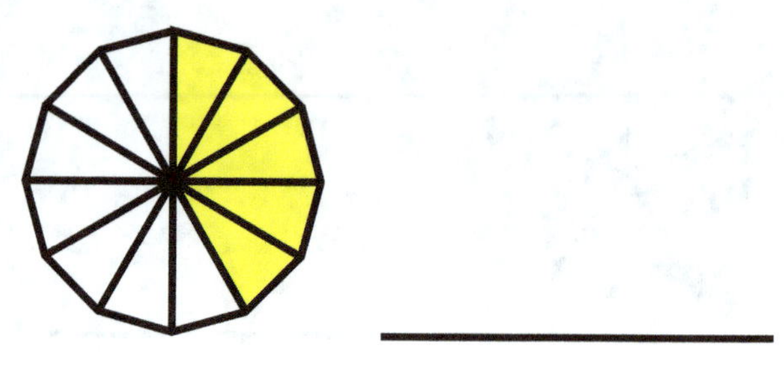
____

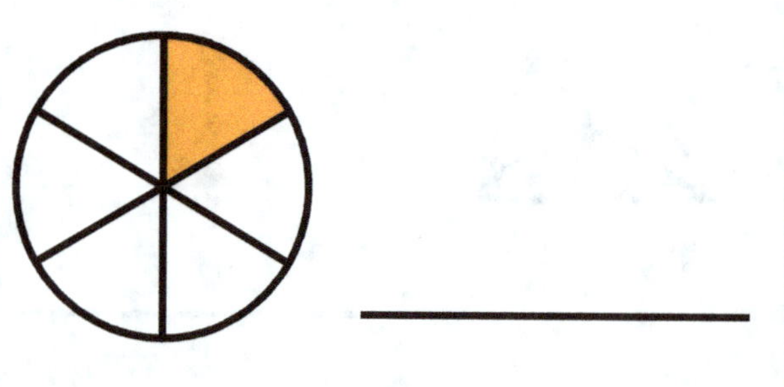
____

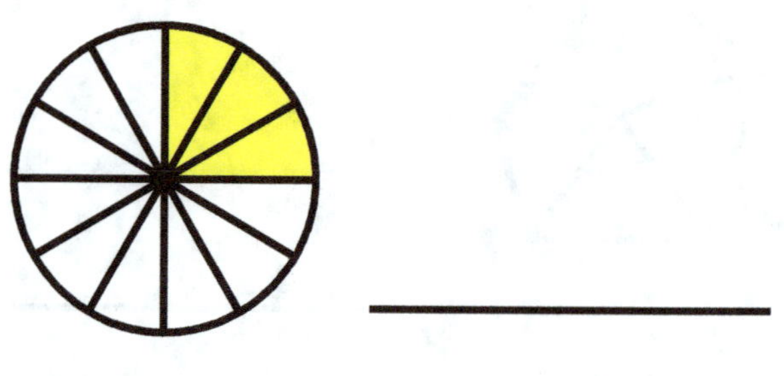
____

Set 5

 __________

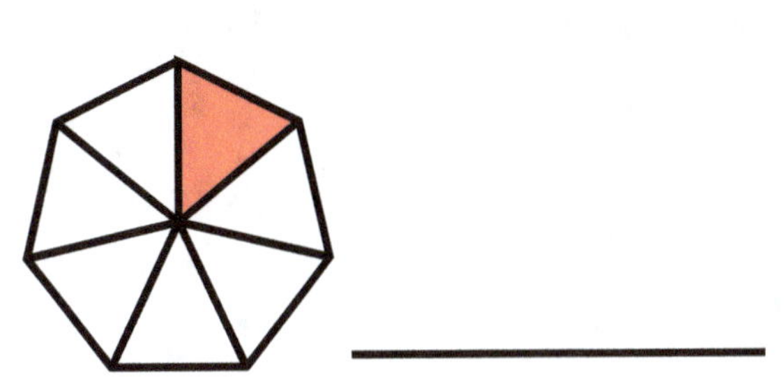 __________

 __________

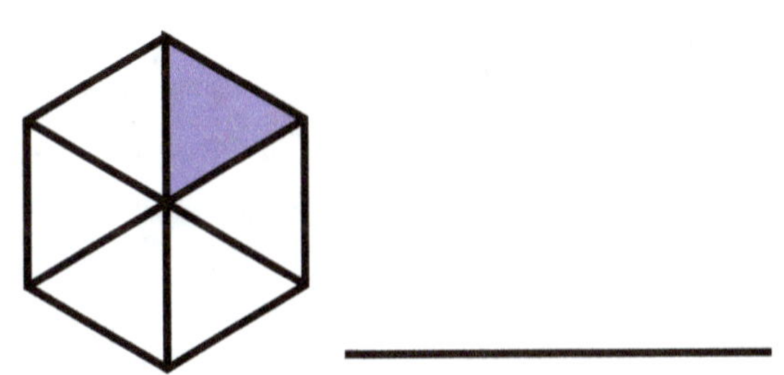 __________

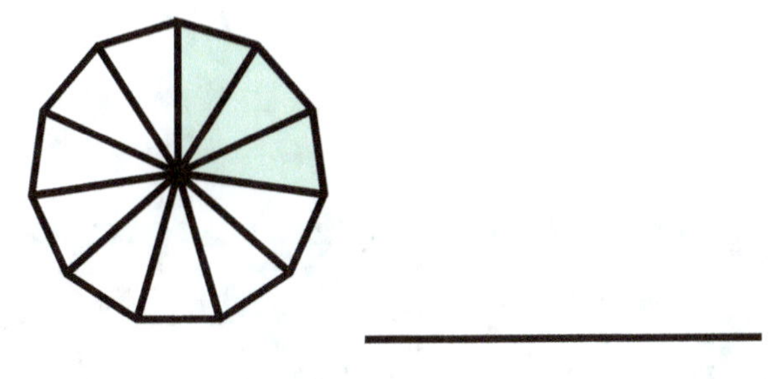 __________

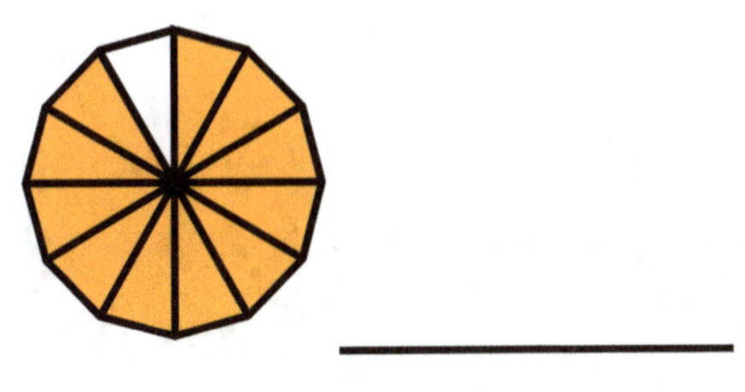 __________

Different Shapes

Set 1

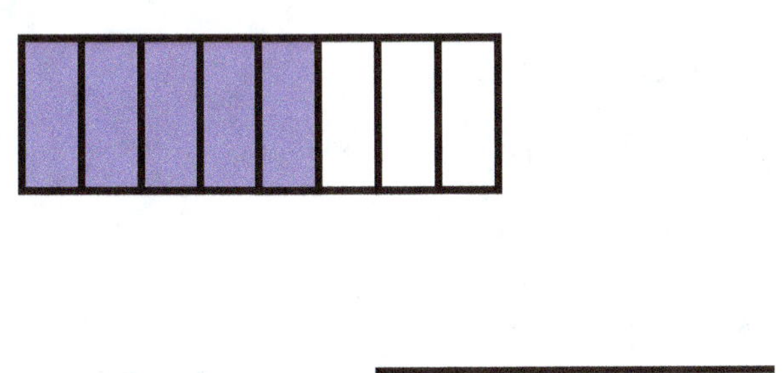

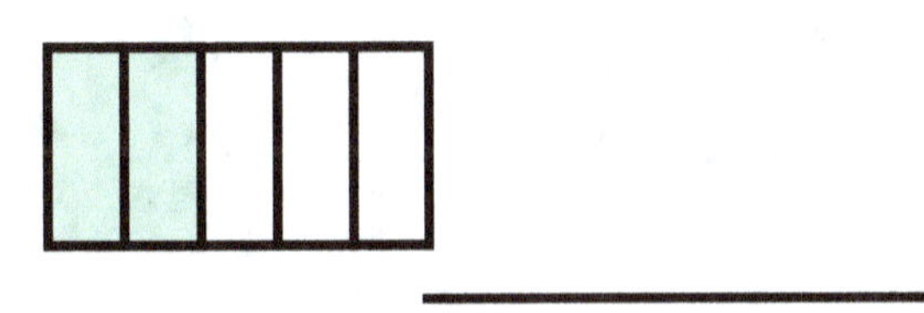

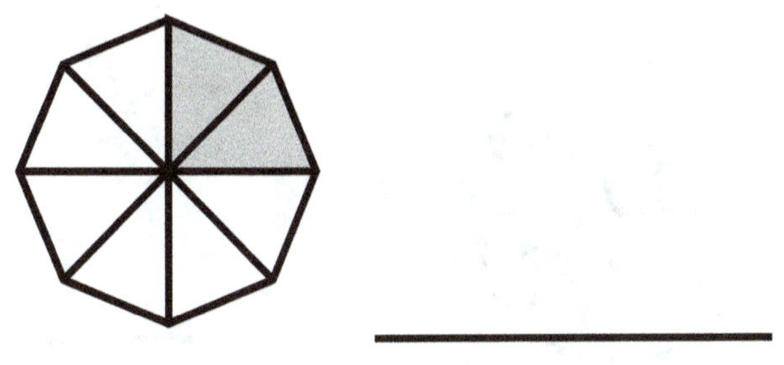

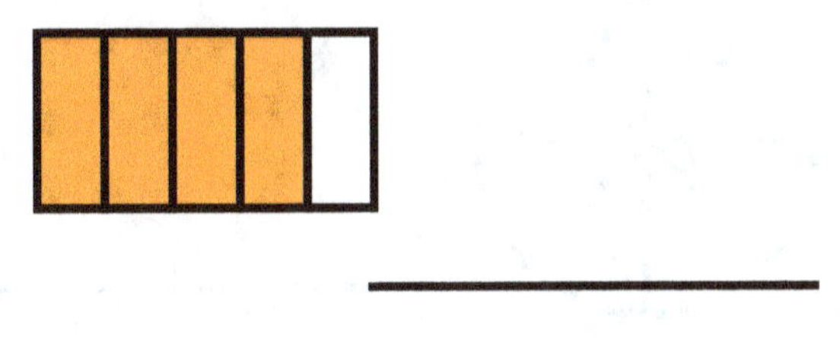

Set 2

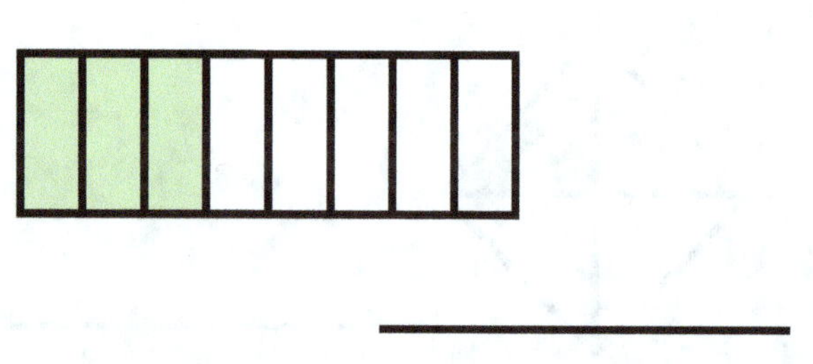 _______

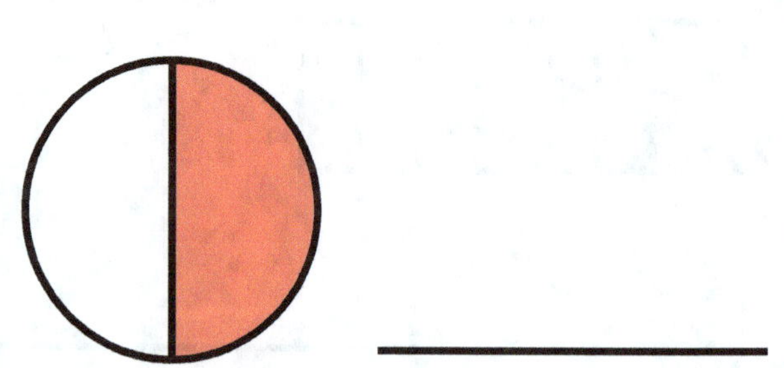 _______

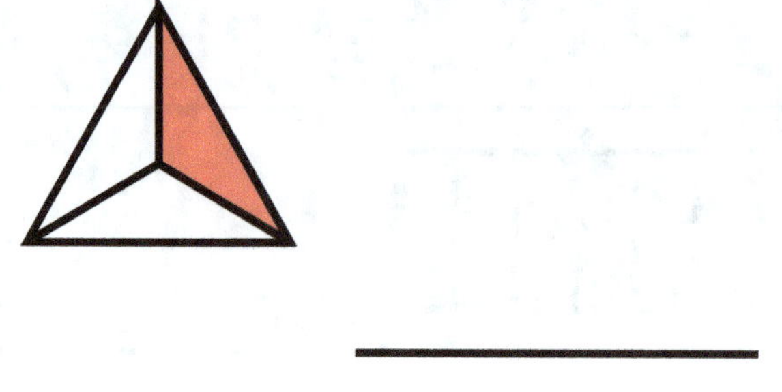 _______

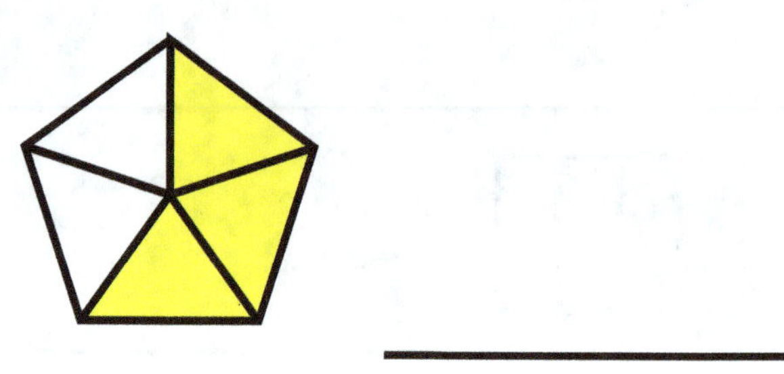 _______

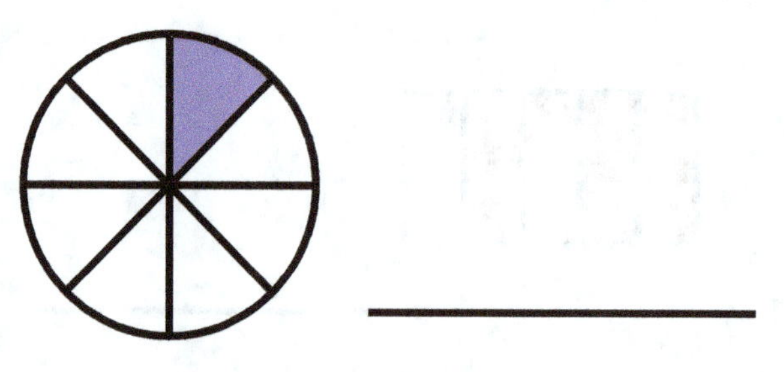 _______

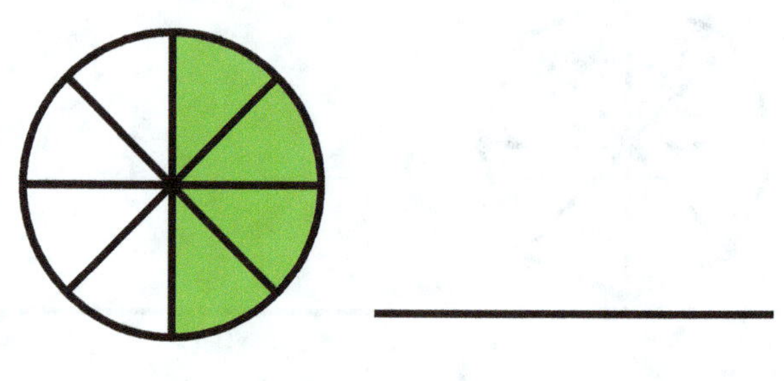 _______

Set 3

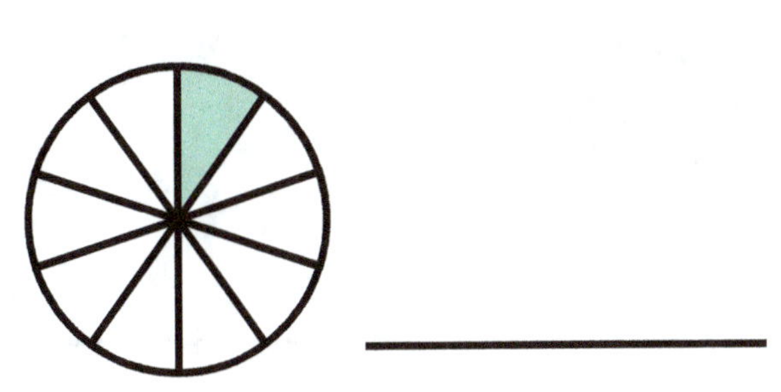 _______

 _______

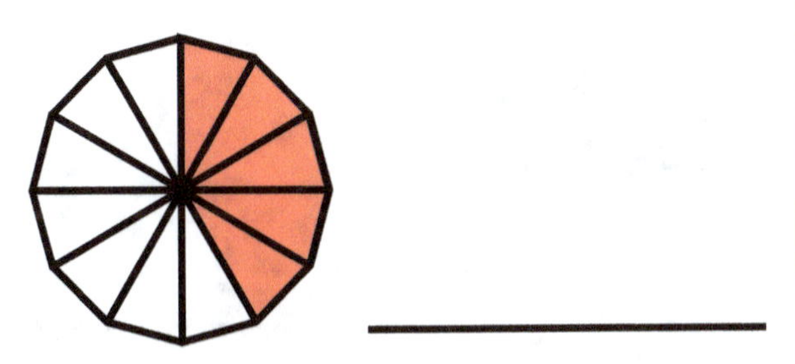 _______

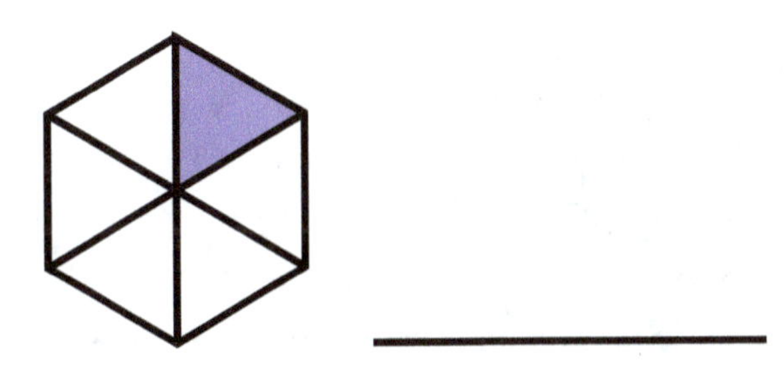 _______

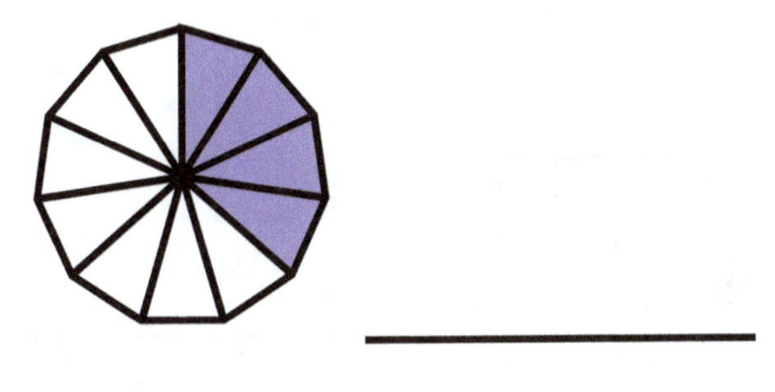 _______

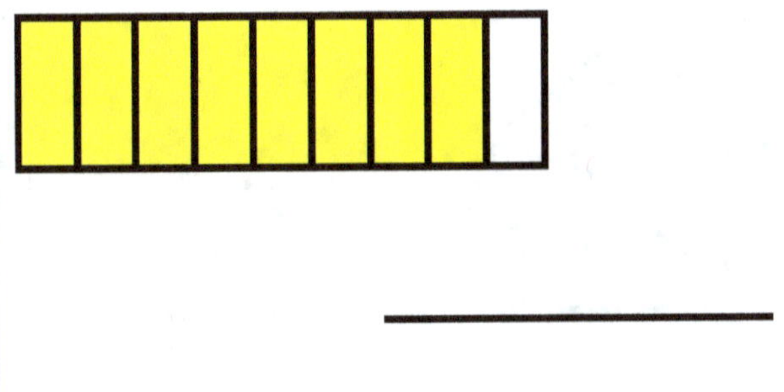 _______

Set 4

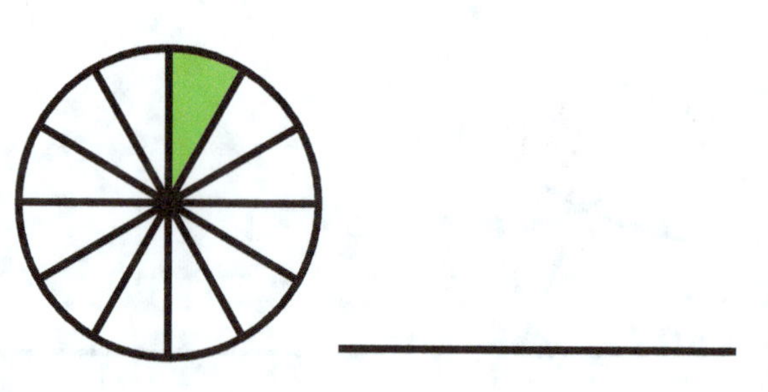 ___________

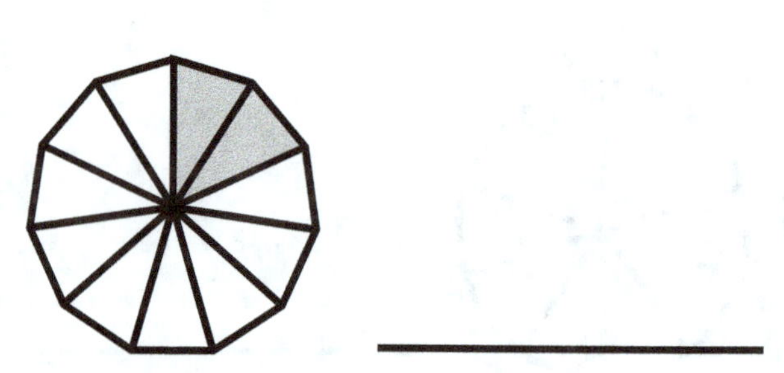 ___________

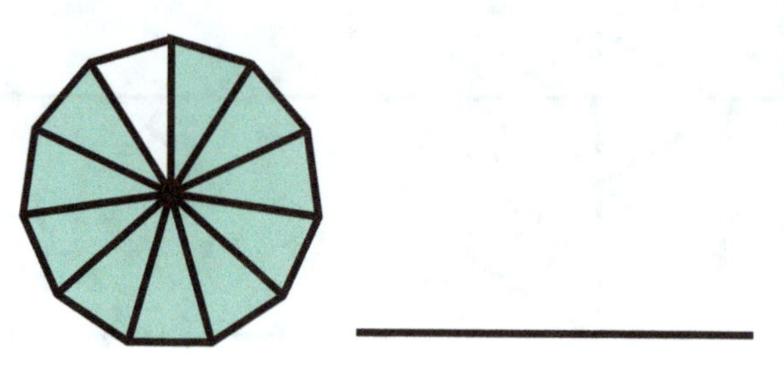 ___________

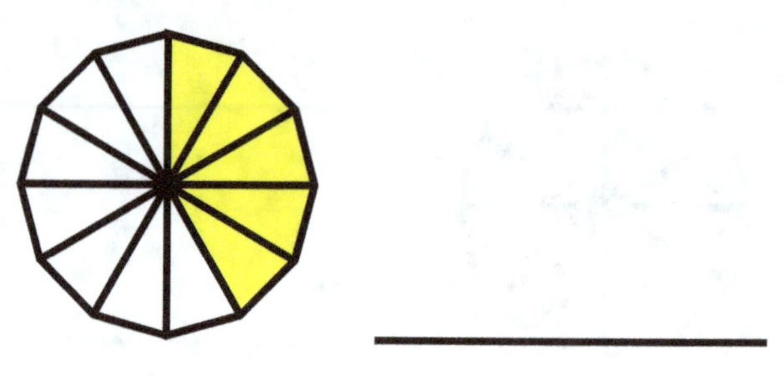 ___________

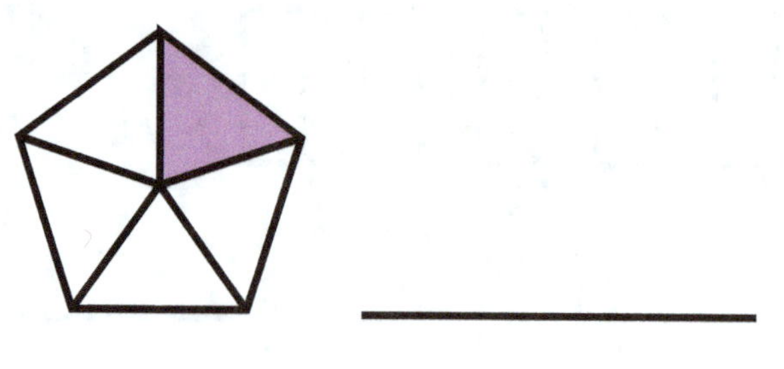 ___________

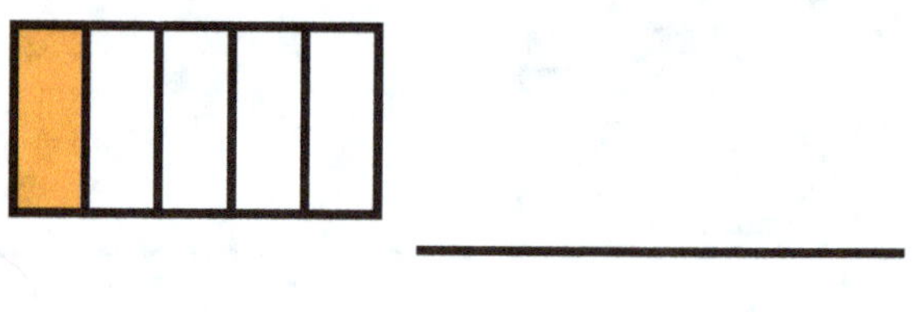 ___________

Set 5

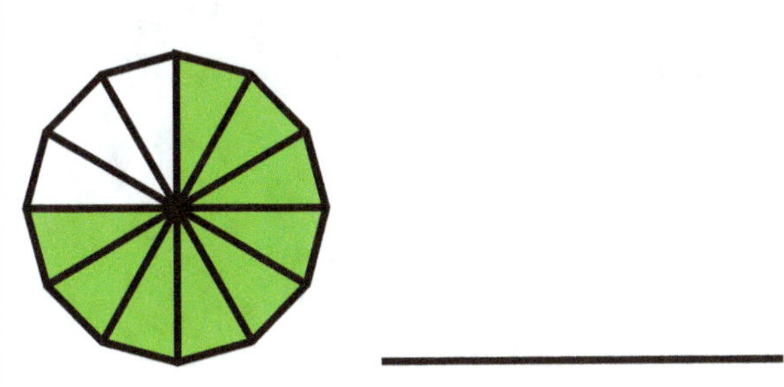 ____________

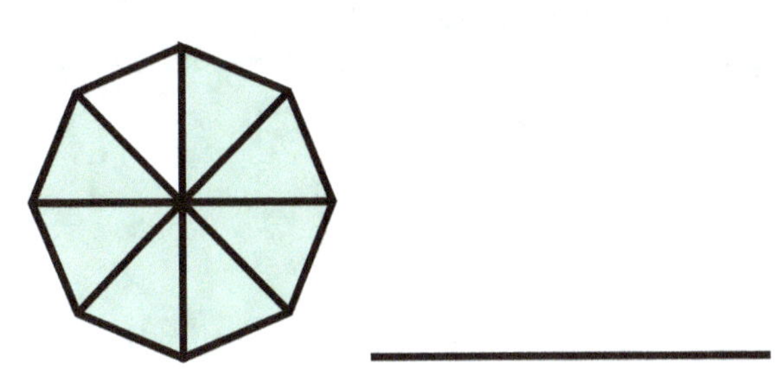 ____________

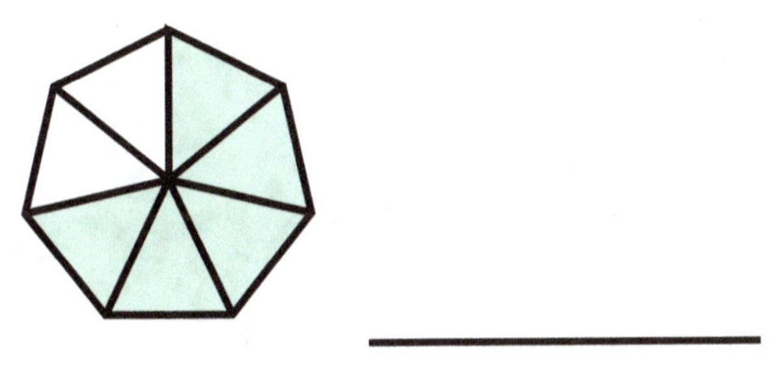 ____________

 ____________

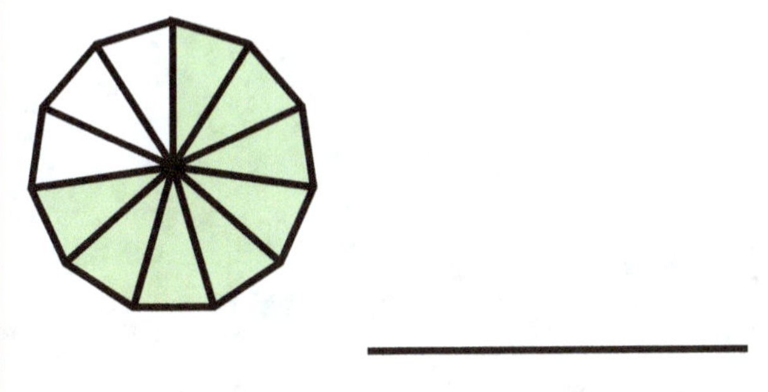 ____________

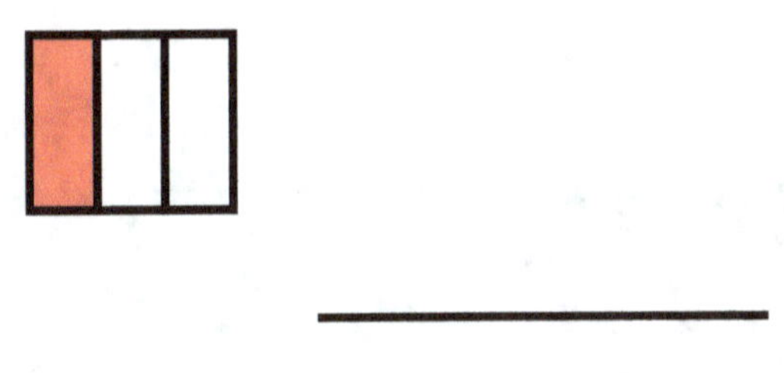 ____________

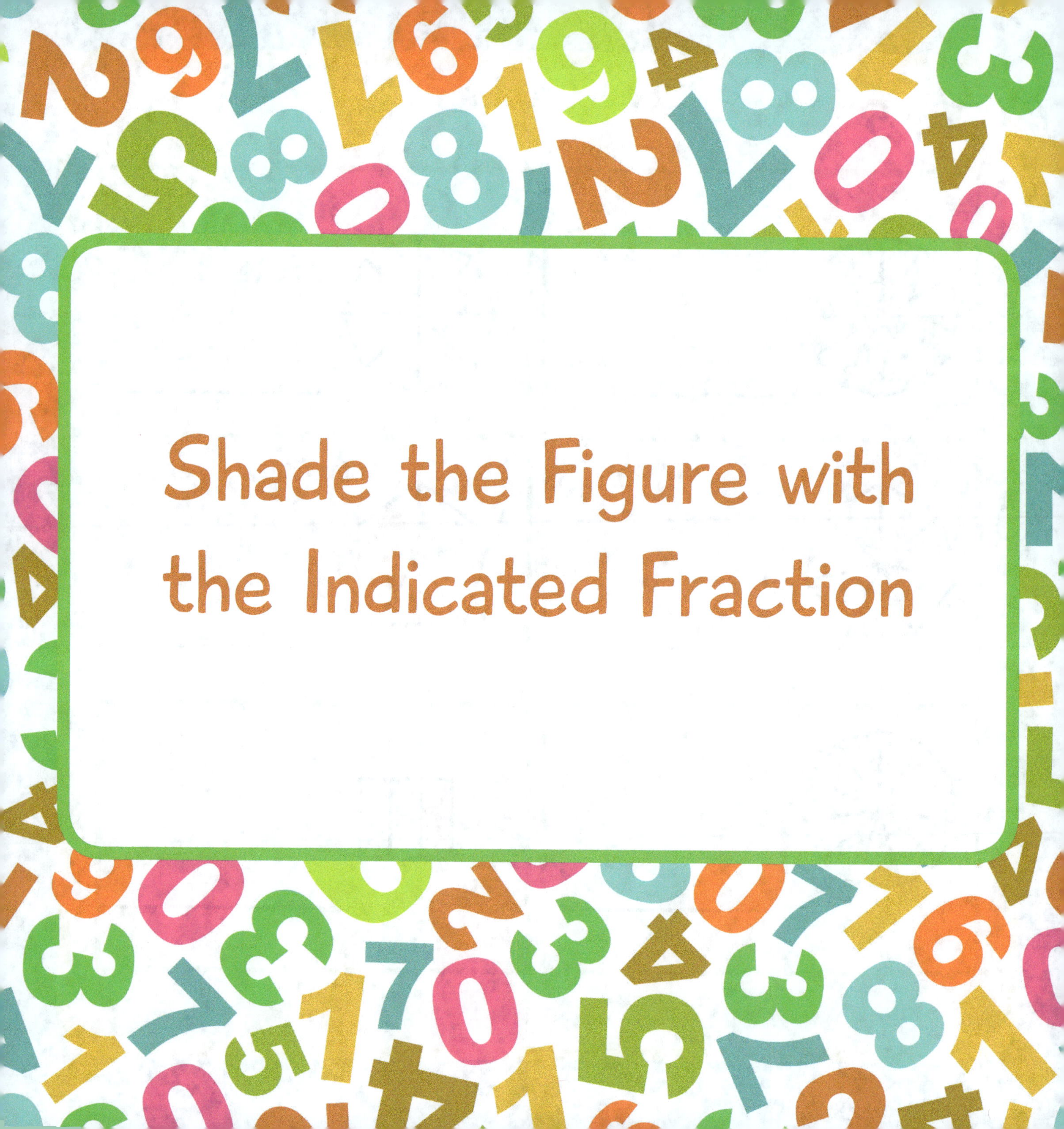

Shade the Figure with the Indicated Fraction

Set 1

<table>
<tr>
<td>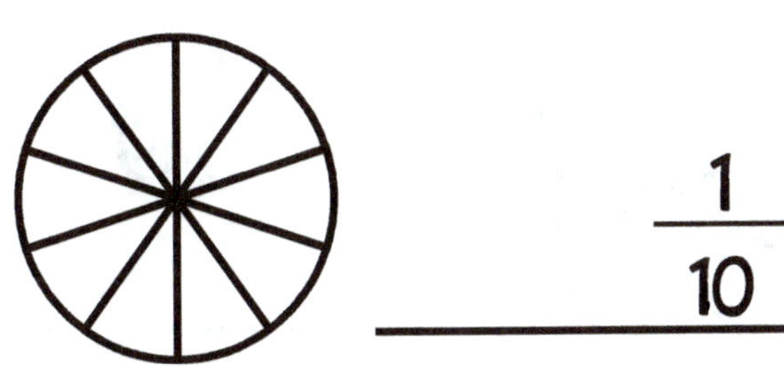
_____ $\dfrac{1}{10}$</td>
<td>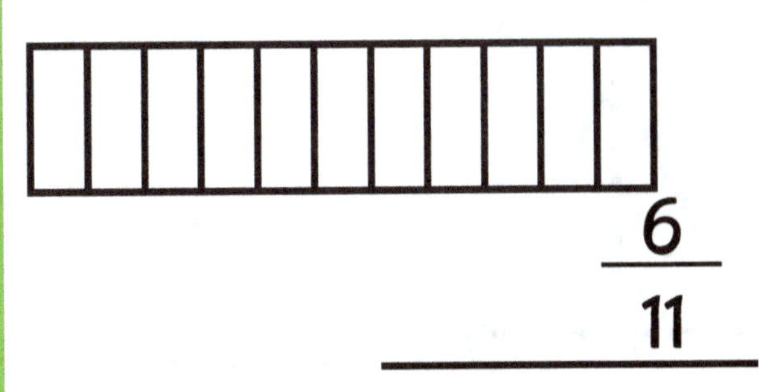
_____ $\dfrac{6}{11}$</td>
</tr>
<tr>
<td>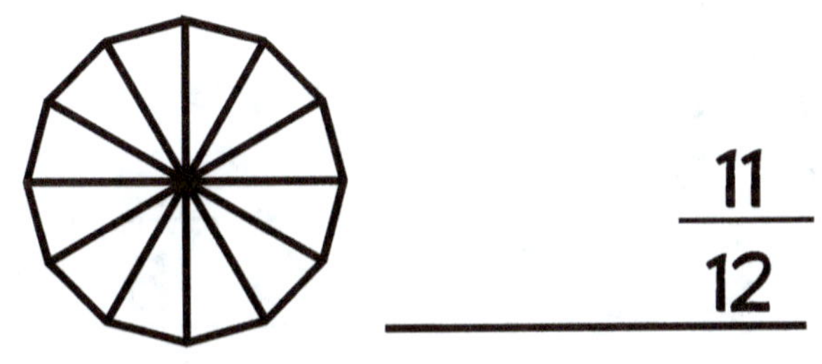
_____ $\dfrac{11}{12}$</td>
<td>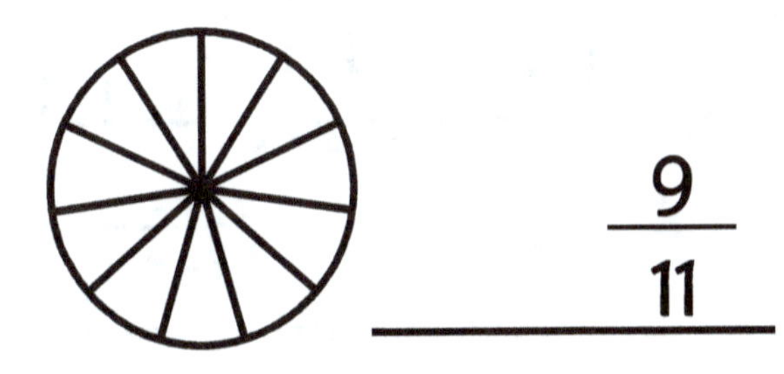
_____ $\dfrac{9}{11}$</td>
</tr>
<tr>
<td>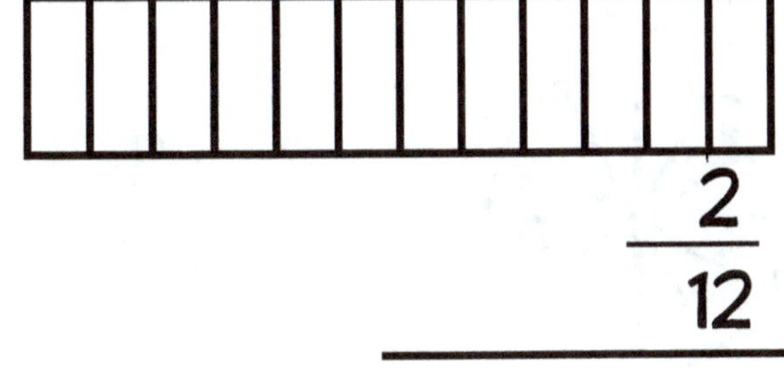
_____ $\dfrac{2}{12}$</td>
<td>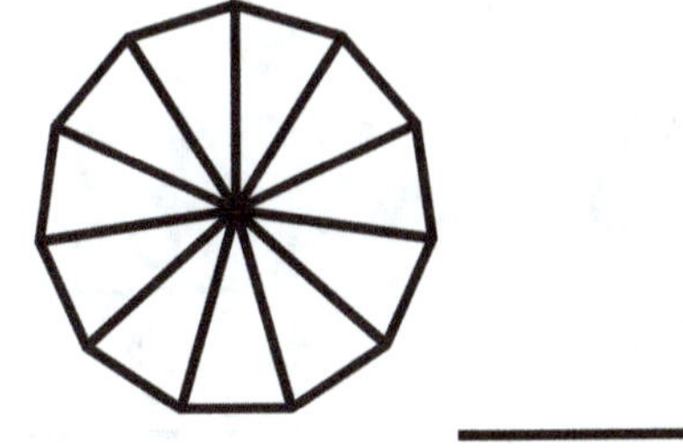
_____ $\dfrac{8}{11}$</td>
</tr>
</table>

Set 2

$$\frac{1}{2}$$

$$\frac{9}{12}$$

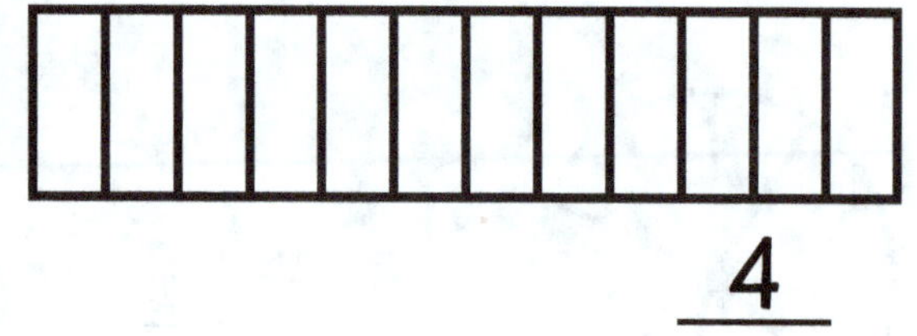

$$\frac{4}{12}$$

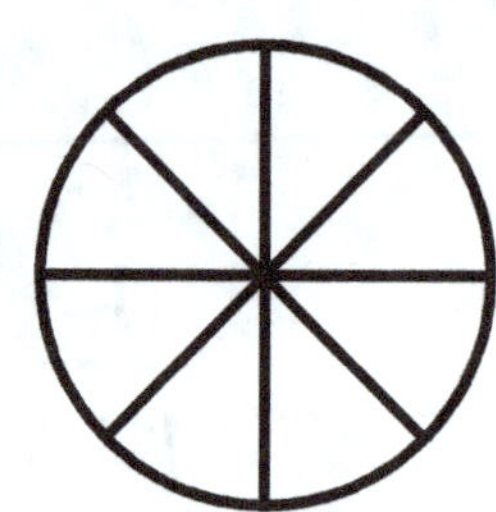

$$\frac{5}{8}$$

$$\frac{6}{9}$$

$$\frac{8}{12}$$

Set 3

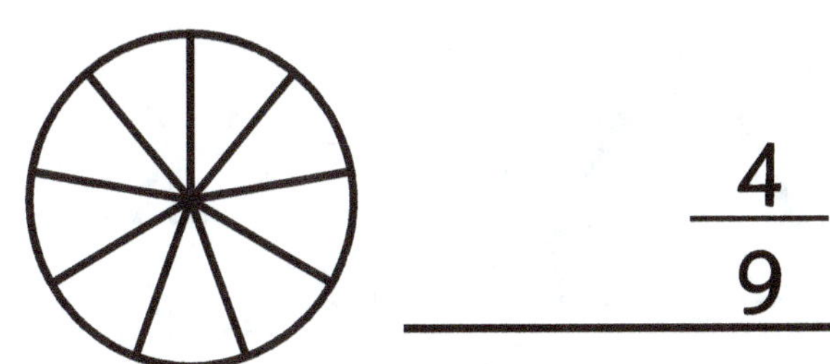

$$\frac{4}{9}$$
_____

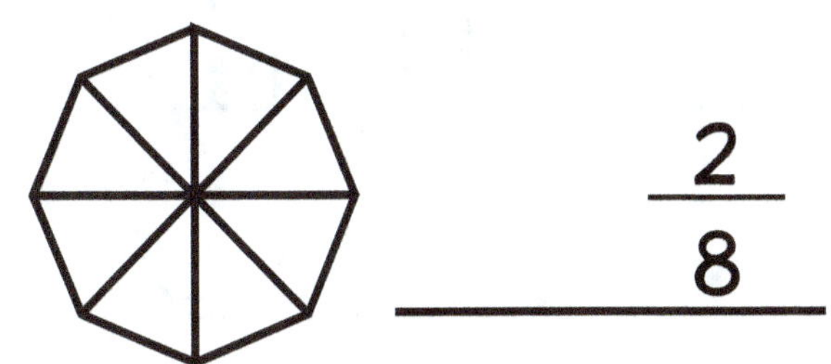

$$\frac{2}{8}$$
_____

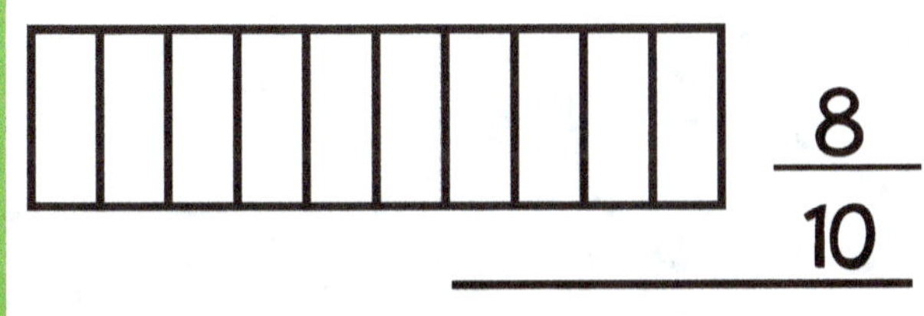

$$\frac{8}{10}$$
_____

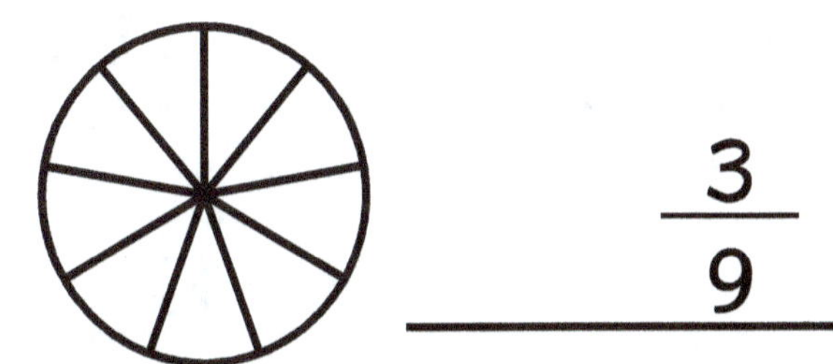

$$\frac{3}{9}$$
_____

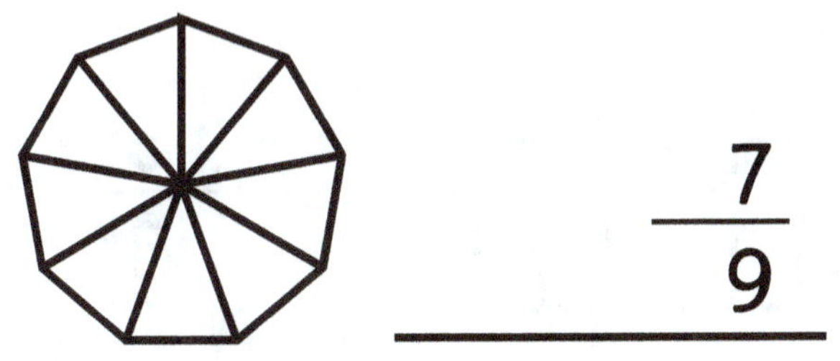

$$\frac{7}{9}$$
_____

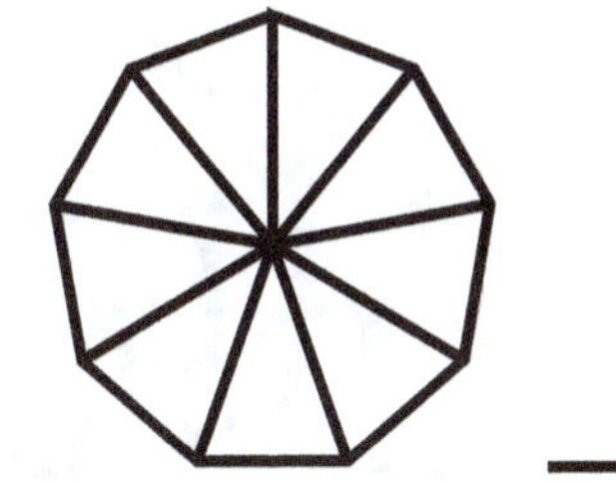

$$\frac{8}{9}$$
_____

Set 4

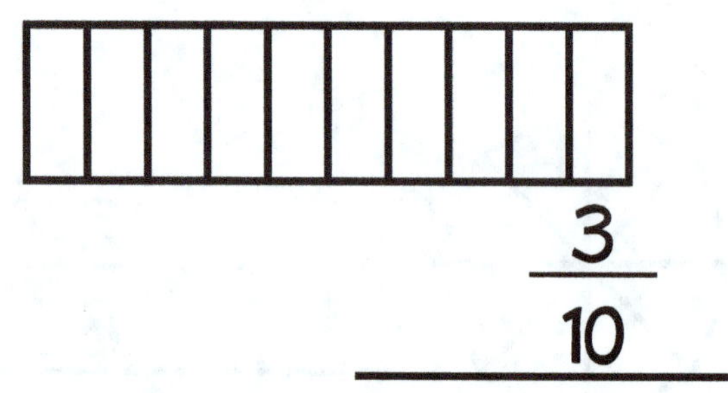

$$\frac{3}{10}$$

____

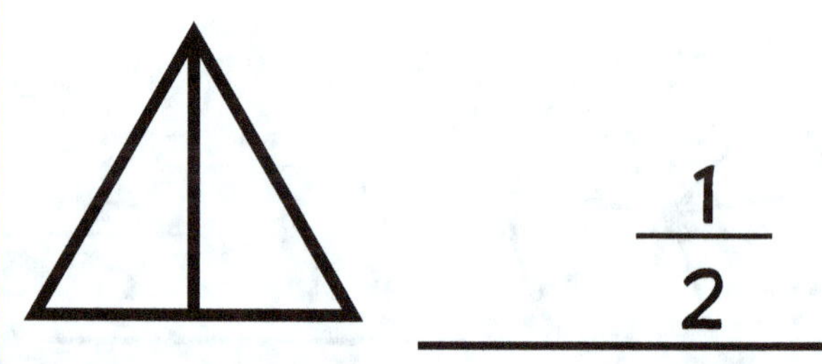

$$\frac{1}{2}$$

____

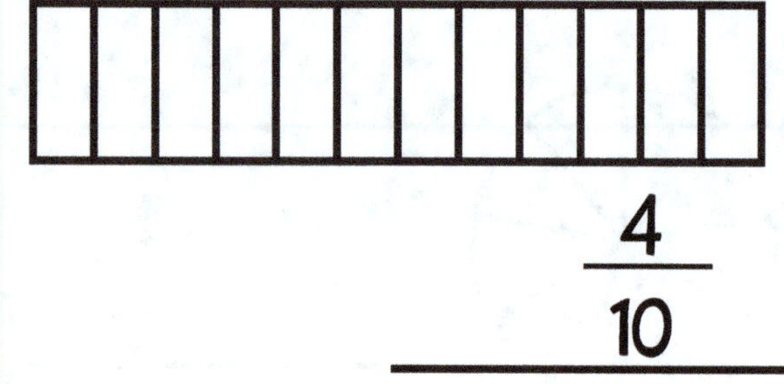

$$\frac{4}{10}$$

____

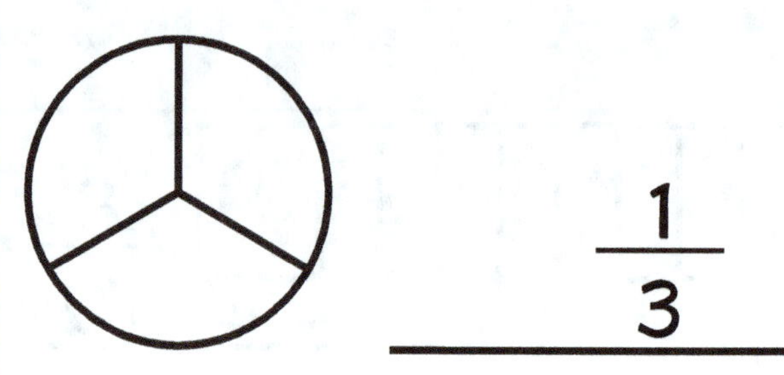

$$\frac{1}{3}$$

____

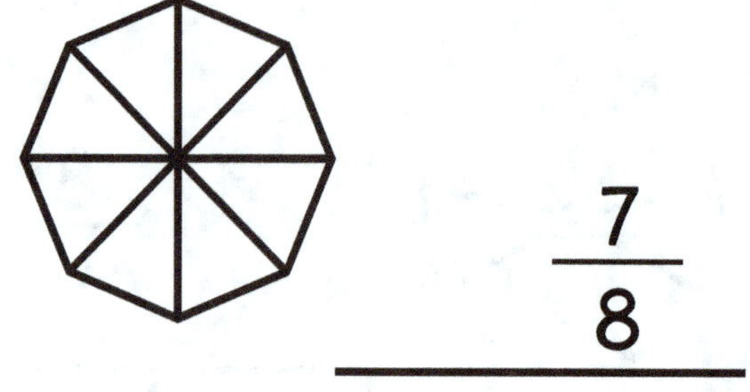

$$\frac{7}{8}$$

____

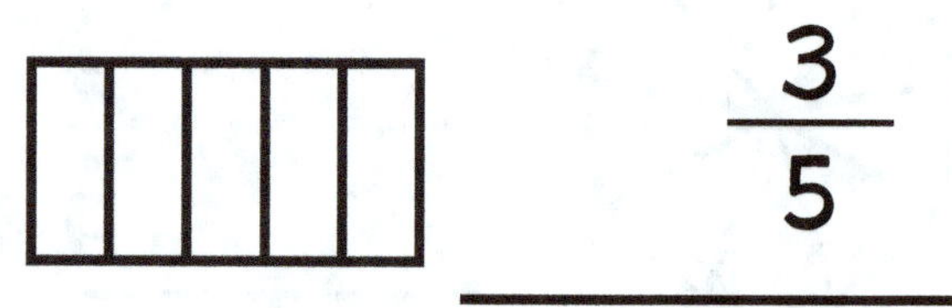

$$\frac{3}{5}$$

____

Set 5

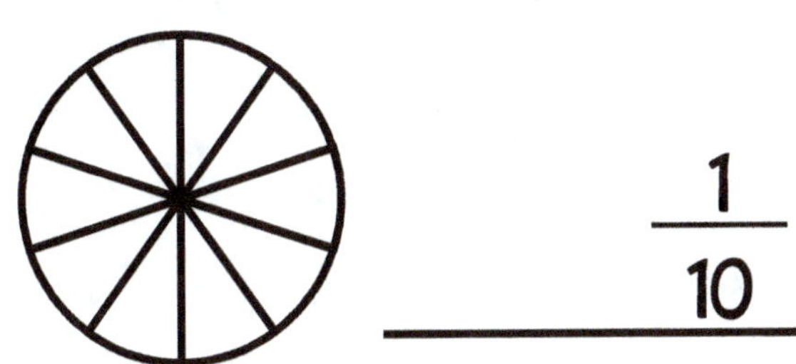

$\dfrac{1}{10}$

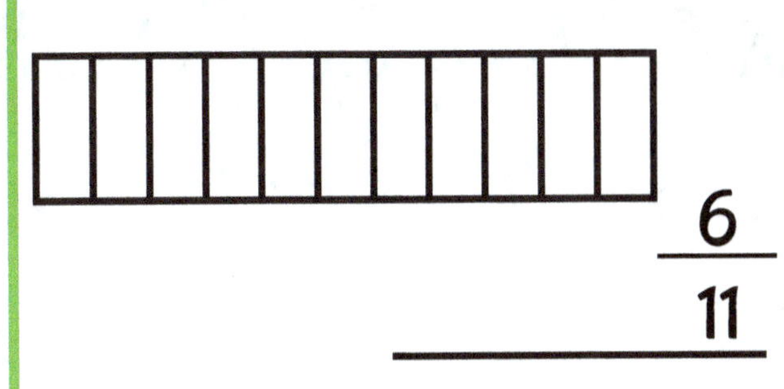

$\dfrac{6}{11}$

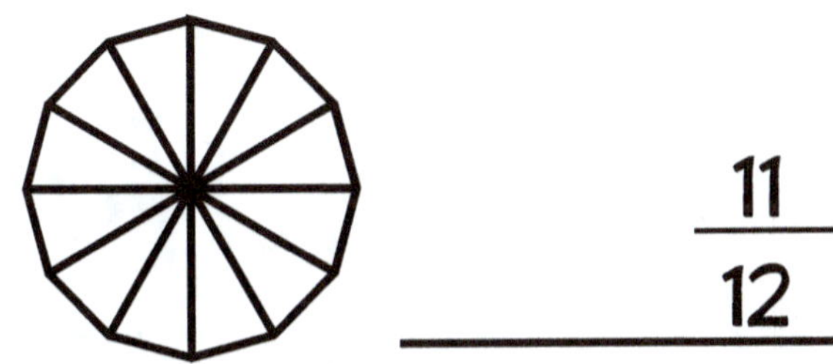

$\dfrac{11}{12}$

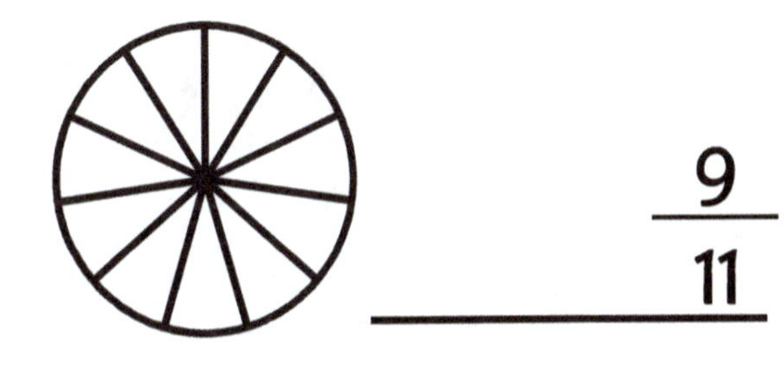

$\dfrac{9}{11}$

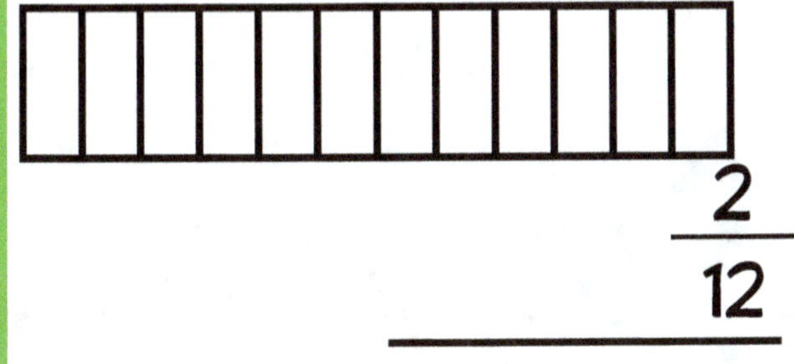

$\dfrac{2}{12}$

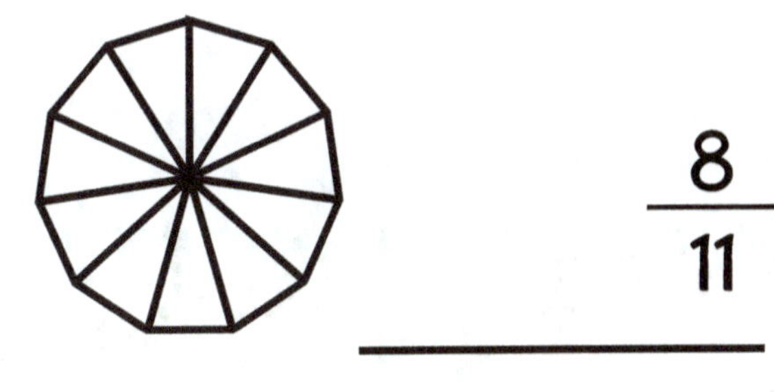

$\dfrac{8}{11}$

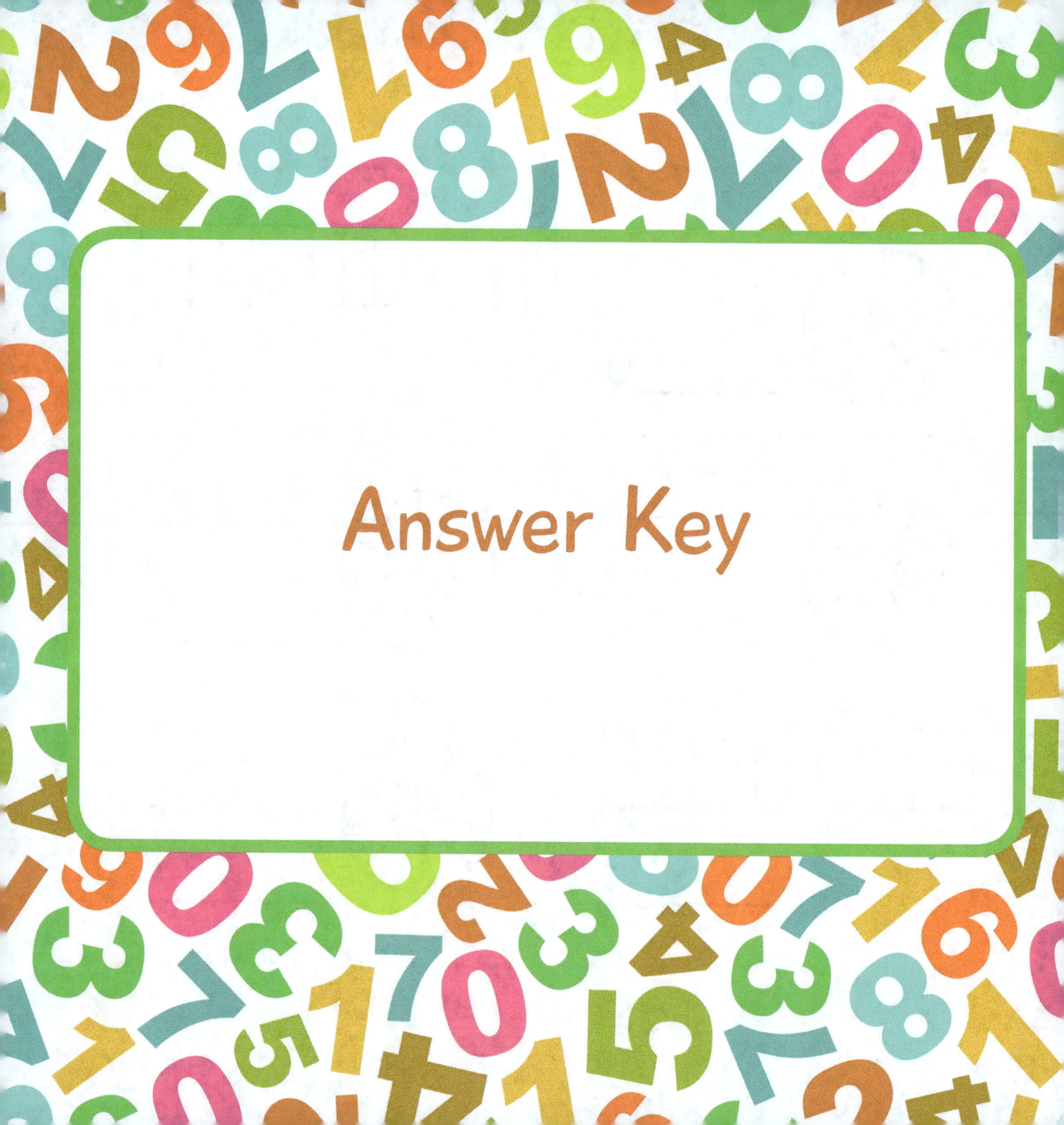

Answer Key

PIE SHAPES

Set 1

$$\frac{3}{4}$$

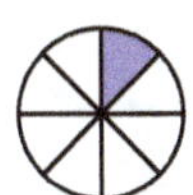
$$\frac{1}{8}$$
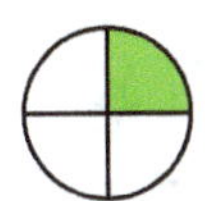

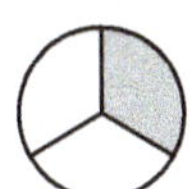
$$\frac{1}{3}$$
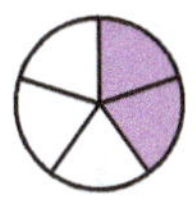

Set 2

$$\frac{7}{8}$$
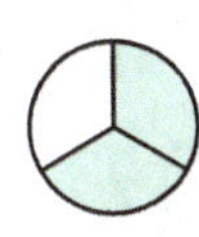
$$\frac{2}{3}$$
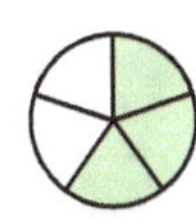
$$\frac{3}{5}$$

$$\frac{1}{4}$$
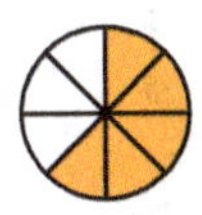
$$\frac{5}{8}$$
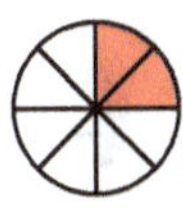
$$\frac{2}{8}$$

$$\frac{2}{5}$$
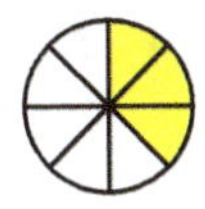
$$\frac{3}{8}$$
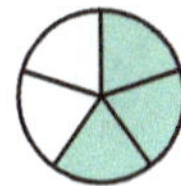
$$\frac{3}{5}$$

Set 3

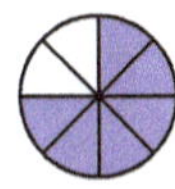
$$\frac{6}{8}$$
Set 1
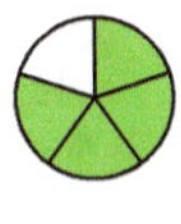

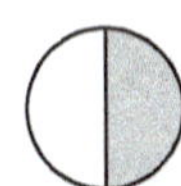
$$\frac{1}{2}$$
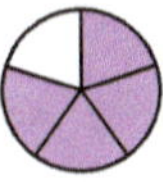

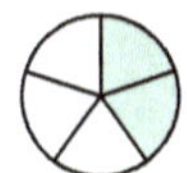
$$\frac{2}{5}$$
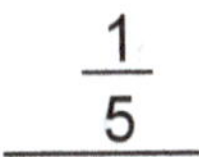

Set 4

$$\frac{4}{5}$$
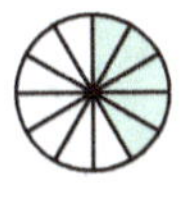
$$\frac{5}{12}$$
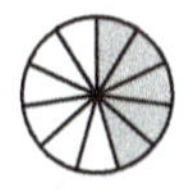
$$\frac{5}{11}$$

$$\frac{4}{5}$$
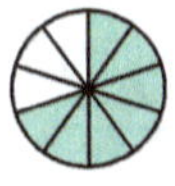
$$\frac{7}{10}$$
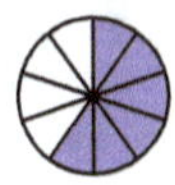
$$\frac{6}{10}$$

$$\frac{1}{5}$$

$$\frac{1}{6}$$

$$\frac{3}{12}$$

Set 5

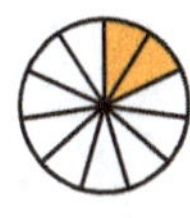
$$\frac{2}{11}$$
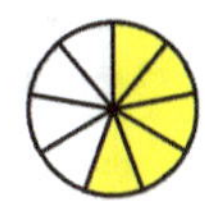
$$\frac{5}{9}$$

$$\frac{4}{7}$$
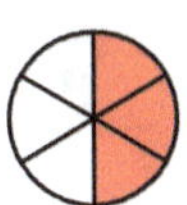
$$\frac{3}{6}$$

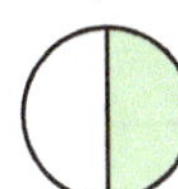
$$\frac{1}{2}$$

$$\frac{2}{10}$$

RECTANGULAR SHAPES

Set 1

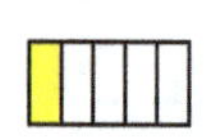 $\dfrac{1}{5}$ 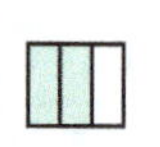 $\dfrac{2}{3}$

 $\dfrac{1}{3}$ 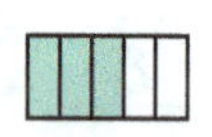 $\dfrac{3}{5}$

 $\dfrac{2}{8}$ 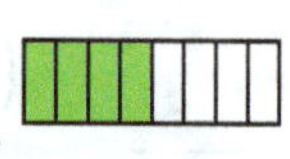 $\dfrac{4}{8}$

Set 2

$\dfrac{2}{5}$ 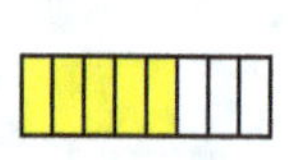 $\dfrac{2}{5}$

$\dfrac{3}{8}$ $\dfrac{1}{2}$

$\dfrac{5}{8}$ $\dfrac{2}{4}$

Set 3

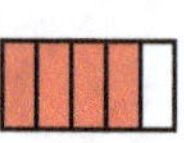 $\dfrac{4}{5}$ 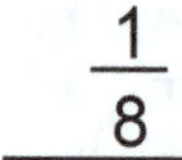 $\dfrac{1}{8}$

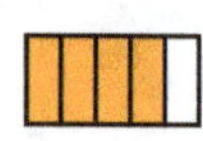 $\dfrac{4}{5}$ $\dfrac{6}{8}$

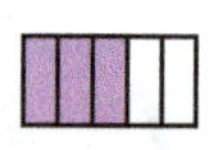 $\dfrac{3}{5}$ $\dfrac{7}{8}$

Set 4

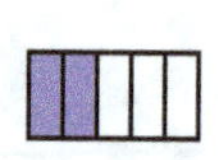 $\dfrac{2}{5}$ 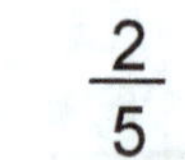 $\dfrac{6}{9}$

$\dfrac{5}{7}$ 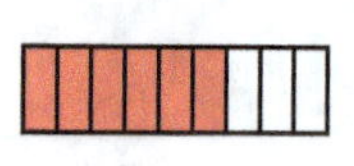 $\dfrac{5}{10}$

 $\dfrac{1}{8}$ 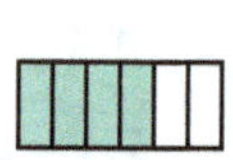 $\dfrac{4}{6}$

Set 5

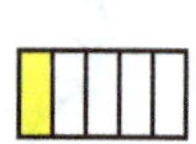 $\dfrac{1}{5}$ $\dfrac{2}{3}$

 $\dfrac{1}{3}$ $\dfrac{3}{5}$

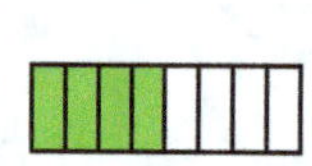 $\dfrac{2}{8}$ $\dfrac{4}{8}$

POLYGONAL SHAPES

Set 1

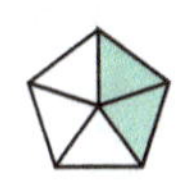 $\dfrac{2}{5}$ 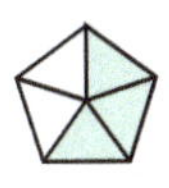 $\dfrac{3}{4}$

 $\dfrac{1}{8}$  $\dfrac{3}{8}$

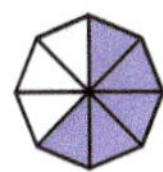 $\dfrac{5}{8}$ 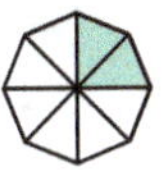 $\dfrac{1}{5}$

Set 2

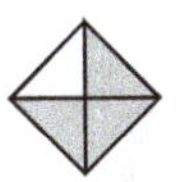 $\dfrac{3}{5}$ 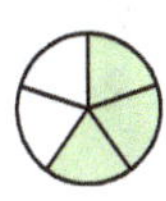 $\dfrac{3}{5}$

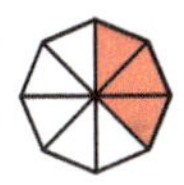 $\dfrac{2}{4}$ 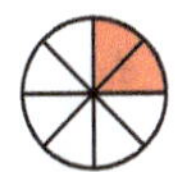 $\dfrac{2}{8}$

 $\dfrac{2}{8}$ 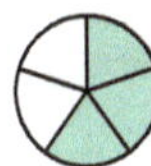 $\dfrac{3}{5}$

Set 3

 $\dfrac{4}{8}$ 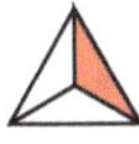 $\dfrac{1}{3}$

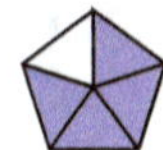 $\dfrac{4}{5}$  $\dfrac{1}{4}$

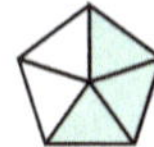 $\dfrac{3}{5}$ 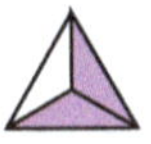 $\dfrac{2}{3}$

Set 4

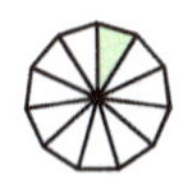 $\dfrac{1}{11}$ 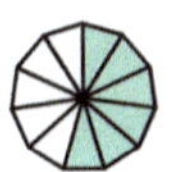 $\dfrac{2}{11}$

 $\dfrac{6}{11}$ $\dfrac{5}{12}$

$\dfrac{1}{6}$ $\dfrac{3}{12}$

Set 5

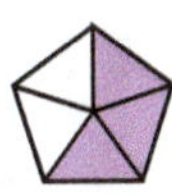 $\dfrac{3}{5}$ 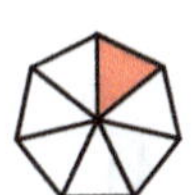 $\dfrac{1}{7}$

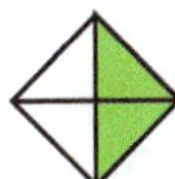 $\dfrac{2}{4}$ 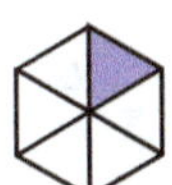 $\dfrac{1}{6}$

 $\dfrac{3}{11}$  $\dfrac{11}{12}$

DIFFERENT SHAPES

Set 1

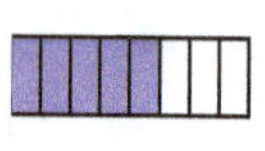 $\dfrac{5}{8}$ 

 $\dfrac{2}{4}$ 

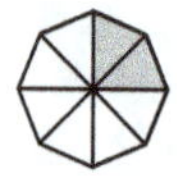 $\dfrac{2}{8}$ 

Set 2

$\dfrac{1}{4}$ 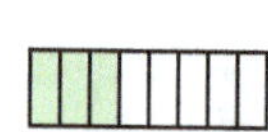 $\dfrac{3}{8}$ 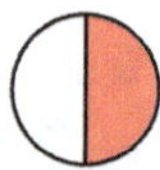 $\dfrac{1}{2}$

$\dfrac{2}{5}$ 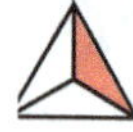 $\dfrac{1}{3}$ 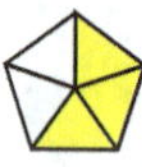 $\dfrac{3}{5}$

$\dfrac{4}{5}$  $\dfrac{1}{8}$  $\dfrac{4}{8}$

Set 3

 $\dfrac{1}{10}$ 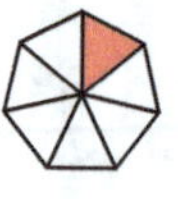

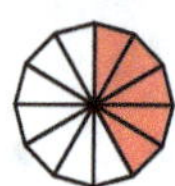 $\dfrac{5}{12}$ 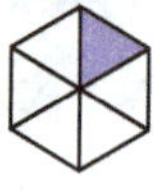

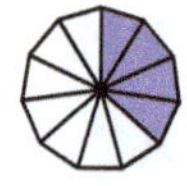 $\dfrac{4}{11}$ 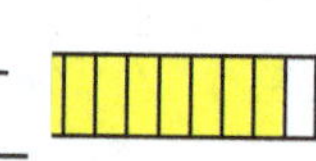

Set 4

$\dfrac{1}{7}$  $\dfrac{1}{12}$ 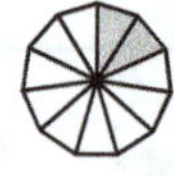 $\dfrac{2}{11}$

$\dfrac{1}{6}$ 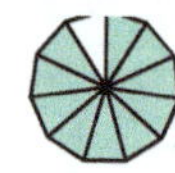 $\dfrac{10}{11}$ 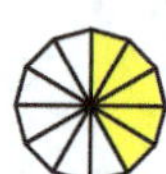 $\dfrac{5}{12}$

$\dfrac{8}{9}$ 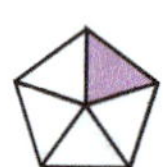 $\dfrac{1}{5}$  $\dfrac{1}{5}$

Set 5

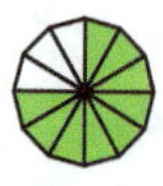 $\dfrac{9}{12}$ 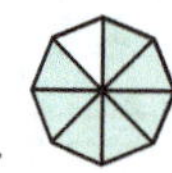 $\dfrac{7}{8}$

 $\dfrac{5}{7}$ 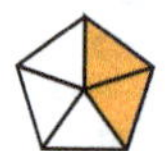 $\dfrac{2}{5}$

 $\dfrac{8}{11}$  $\dfrac{1}{3}$

Set 1

 $\dfrac{1}{10}$ 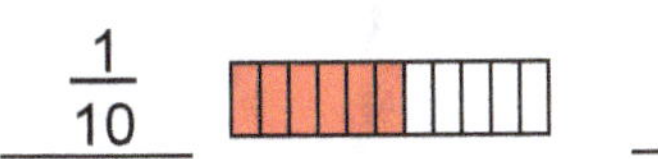 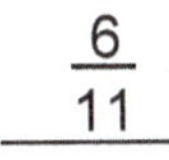 $\dfrac{6}{11}$

 $\dfrac{11}{12}$ 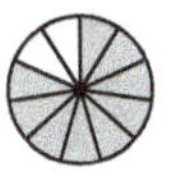 $\dfrac{9}{11}$

 $\dfrac{2}{12}$ 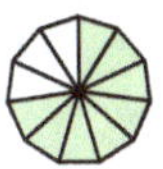 $\dfrac{8}{11}$

Set 2

 $\dfrac{1}{2}$ 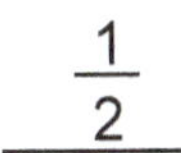 $\dfrac{9}{12}$

 $\dfrac{4}{12}$  $\dfrac{5}{8}$

 $\dfrac{6}{9}$ 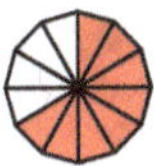 $\dfrac{8}{12}$

Set 3

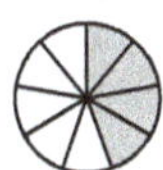 $\dfrac{4}{9}$ 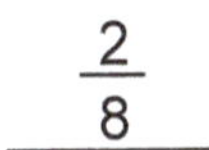 $\dfrac{2}{8}$

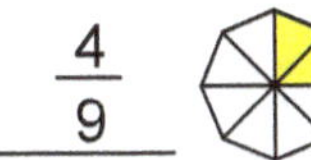 $\dfrac{8}{10}$  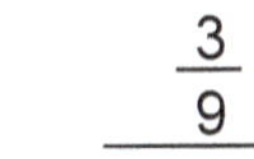 $\dfrac{3}{9}$

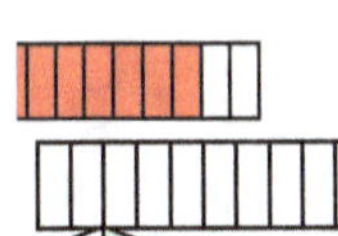 $\dfrac{7}{9}$ 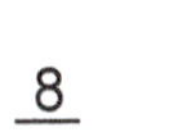 $\dfrac{8}{9}$

Set 4

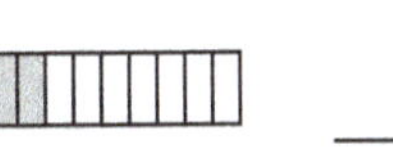 $\dfrac{3}{10}$  $\dfrac{1}{2}$

 $\dfrac{4}{11}$ 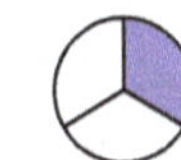 $\dfrac{1}{3}$

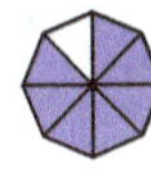 $\dfrac{7}{8}$ 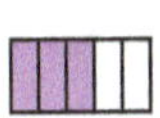 $\dfrac{3}{5}$

Set 5

 $\dfrac{1}{10}$ 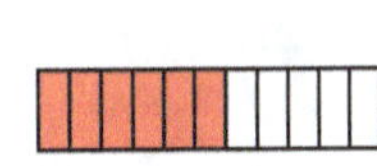 $\dfrac{6}{11}$

 $\dfrac{11}{12}$ 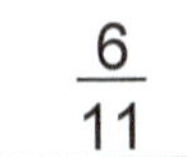 $\dfrac{9}{11}$

 $\dfrac{2}{12}$ 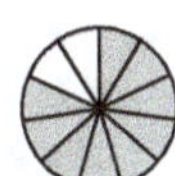 $\dfrac{8}{11}$